THE EASTERN EUROPE COLLECTION

CZECHOSLOVAKIA

A Survey of Economic and Social Conditions

Edited by
Josef Gruber

ARNO PRESS & THE NEW YORK TIMES
New York - 1971

Reprint Edition 1971 by Arno Press Inc.

LC# 76-135810

ISBN 0-405-02752-4

The Eastern Europe Collection
ISBN for complete set: 0-405-02730-3

Manufactured in the United States of America

CZECHOSLOVAKIA

A Survey of Economic and Social Conditions

THE MACMILLAN COMPANY
NEW YORK · BOSTON · CHICAGO · DALLAS
ATLANTA · SAN FRANCISCO

MACMILLAN & CO., LIMITED
LONDON · BOMBAY · CALCUTTA
MELBOURNE

THE MACMILLAN CO. OF CANADA, LTD.
TORONTO

CZECHOSLOVAKIA

A Survey of Economic and Social Conditions

EDITED BY

DR. JOSEF GRUBER

PROFESSOR OF ECONOMICS AT THE CHARLES UNIVERSITY
IN PRAGUE

Translated from Czech Manuscripts
by
A. BROŽ, S. V. KLÍMA AND J. J. KRÁL

New York
THE MACMILLAN COMPANY
1924

Published September, 1924.

PRINTED IN THE UNITED STATES OF AMERICA.

INTRODUCTORY NOTES ON THE PRESENT SOCIAL AND INDUSTRIAL CONDITIONS

Dr. Václav Verunáč, Director of the Institute for Industrial Economics, Masaryk's Academy of Labor, Prague

The political upheaval of October 28, 1918, through which Czechoslovakia was established as an independent State, may not mark the inauguration of a new era in the economic and social life of the country, yet an important beginning has been made toward a readjustment of the war conditions in conformity with the new political state of affairs After the establishment of the Czechoslovak Republic the effect of the abnormal conditions prevailing during the war was felt in an increased measure, especially in wages, prices, and general social conditions. The misery and exhaustion of the masses, the weakened ties of morality on the one hand, and the increased materialism on the other, all these prepared the ground for the revolutionary ideas which had been preached at various periods in the neighboring countries of Russia, Hungary, Germany and Austria. Thanks to the sound common sense of Czech workmen and to their nationalist feeling, the communist agitators have not succeeded in winning the Czech workmen for their extreme demands, or at least not to the same extent as in the neighboring countries. The influence of the

Russian social revolution was felt acutely, as is quite natural in the present intercourse of nations, and did not remain without effect on the social and the labor questions, but was never strong enough to shake the economic structure of the State. The spirit of enterprise was, of course, to a certain extent weakened, but the political consolidation and the authority of the government made steady progress, so that at present the State is fairly well consolidated.

The Czechoslovak Republic has taken over the greater part of the industries of the former Hapsburg Monarchy, although its territory represents only 22 per cent and its population 26 per cent of that of the defunct Empire. The industries taken over include 92 per cent of the sugar factories, 65 per cent of the breweries, 95 per cent of the malt factories, 50 per cent of the liquor industry, 90 per cent of the glass industry, 70 per cent of the leather industry, and the greater part of the textile industry, the latter employing about 270,000 workmen.

The various branches of the textile industry are distributed as follows:

(*a*) The cotton industry in Austria-Hungary comprised 4,941,000 spindles, of which 3,565,000 spindles, or nearly 75 per cent, remained in Czechoslovakia. There are in Czechoslovakia 130,000 mechanical looms, or about 90 per cent of the number of mechanical looms in the former monarchy. Besides this, there are 20 to 30 thousand hand-looms. Of the 220 pattern-printing machines of the former monarchy, 170 are now in Czechoslovakia.

(*b*) The woolen industry comprises 92 per cent of

the looms and 65 per cent of the spindles for carded yarn and 74 per cent of the spindles for worsted yarn, of the former monarchy. This proportion represents about 34,000 looms and 800,000 spindles for carded yarn and 400,000 spindles for worsted yarn. For the full employment of this industry about 31,000 tons of wool are required. As a sheep will give about 2 kilograms of wool annually, the home supply in 1919 amounted to about 1,440 tons of raw wool, *i.e.*, about 4.6 per cent of the home consumption.

(*c*) The flax industry comprises 26 spinning mills with 284,793 spindles, that is, 97 per cent of all the spindles of the former monarchy, and 140 weaving mills with 11,000 mechanical and 5,690 hand looms.

(*d*) The jute industry comprises 9 spinning mills with 34,844 spindles which consume 40,000 tons of jute annually. These spinning mills are run in connection with weaving mills having 1,700 looms; there are also 11 independent weaving mills with 1,880 looms, so that the jute industry comprises altogether 3,580 looms.

(*e*) The silk industry comprises 53 mills and 14,000 looms.

Czechoslovakia has also taken over about 75 per cent of the Austro-Hungarian chemical industry, 70 per cent of the paper industry, and 80 per cent of the building and the ceramic industries.

In 1915 Austria had 282 coal mines of which 219, or 79 per cent, were situated in the Bohemian territories. The total output in 1915 amounted to 38,353,-628 metric tons, of which 16,289,793 metric tons was bituminous coal and 22,063,835 metric tons lignite or brown coal. Of this total output Bohemia, Moravia and Silesia produced 14,464,432 metric tons of bituminous coal and 18,148,528 metric tons of lignite, a total of 32,614,960 metric tons, or 85 per cent of the total output of coal in former Austria-Hungary.

In 1915, 105,958 miners were employed, of whom 81,816, *i.e.*, 72 per cent, were in the Czech territories. In 1921 the number of mining concerns increased from 365 to 369 and the number of miners to 127,000.

This short survey of the principal Czechoslovak industries shows clearly that Czechoslovakia is an exporting State par excellence and needs foreign markets. Hence the demand of Czechoslovak manufacturers for the removal of all obstacles standing in the way of free trade.

Out of the thirteen and a half million of Czechoslovakia's inhabitants two and a quarter million are actively employed in the mining and the manufacturing industries and two and a half million in agriculture.

According to the reports of the State Statistical Bureau (Nos. 6 and 31, 1923), the number of persons engaged in agriculture and industry in 1921 was as follows:

	Agriculture	Industry
Bohemia	961,339	1,367,671
Moravia and Silesia	560,207	593,294
Slovakia	751,155	227,220
Carpathian Ruthenia	152,267	24,287
Total	2,424,968	2,212,472

Politically, the Czechoslovak workmen are organized chiefly in the socialist parties. The trade unions are affiliated with two central bodies: the Federation of Czechoslovak Trade Unions, with 675,625 members, and the Czechoslovak Labor Community, with 298,117 members at the end of 1921. Beside these two associations there is a Federation of German Trade Unions, with 372,027 members, an Association of Christian workers with 72,544 members, and several smaller groups of organized labor.

The organizations of the employers are associated in the Central Federation of Czechoslovak Manufacturers and in the Federation of German Manufacturers. Recently there has been established a Confederation of Employers' Organizations, including manufacturers, merchants, bankers, and farmers. A similar institution is the Central Committee of the Czechoslovak Industries.

The relations between employers and employees are, on the whole, satisfactory. Immediately after the war the differences between employers and workmen were, of course, far greater, but under the pressure of the prevailing industrial crisis both sides have learned the value of cooperation, and industrial disputes have been reduced to a minimum. The year 1919 and the first half of 1920 mark the end of the abnormal postwar period which was characterized by a rapid increase of prices and wages, by constant wage disputes, by complaints of coal shortage, diminished productivity, etc. The second half of 1920, however, marks the complete liquidation of war conditions. The stabilization of the Czechoslovak crown made possible the stabilization of wages and prices also, and the foreign trade was freed from the uncertainties of calculation.

As a result of the depreciation of the crown, wages

in various industries had increased from 1913 to 1920 as follows:

In the chemical industries, 500 per cent; in the clothing industries, 900 per cent; in the textile, paper, and leather industries, 900 to 1000 per cent; in the food industries, 1000 per cent; in the furniture industry, 1100 per cent; in the iron, building, and other industries, 1000 to 1300 per cent.

The prices of foodstuffs and other necessaries increased 1384 per cent in the same period.

The index numbers of the State Statistical Bureau for 1921 and 1922 show the following movement of retail prices since 1913 (July, 1914, prices = 100):

1921

	Jan.	Feb.	March	April	May	June
I. Foodstuffs, fuel, oil, and soap	1643	1494	1423	1450	1456	1445
II. Clothes, footwear, hats	2878	2803	2566	2349	2137	1898

	July	Aug.	Sept.	Oct.	Nov.	Dec.
I. Foodstuffs, feul, oil, and soap	1346	1362	1476	1519	1551	1544
II. Clothes, footwear, hats	1865	1877	2019	2086	2087	2052

1922

	Jan.	Feb.	March	June	Aug.	Sept.
I. Foodstuffs, fuel, oil, and soap	1444	1461	1414	1475	1290	1105
II. Clothes, footwear, hats	2053	1960	1882	1736	1614	1409

During the war, a so-called "social wage" was introduced, a wage increasing according to the number of the members of a family. In the mining industry such social bonuses amounted to from 14 to 42 per cent of the basic wage. After the war the "social wage," based upon the number of the members of a family and not on the skill of the worker, was gradually abolished. With the steady increase in the buying power of the crown since the beginning of 1922 a gradual reduction of wages has taken place. This reduction varies from 10 to 20 per cent.

Owing to various causes, the output per workman declined after the war, but has regained the prewar standard since 1922. The effect of the eight-hour working day on the output has not yet been ascertained.

Working conditions, so far as not determined by the law, are regulated by contracts between employers and the labor unions. Both employers and employees have recognized the advantages of contracts, and the working conditions in nearly all branches of the industry are now regulated by agreements.

Immediately after the war, especially in 1919, wage disputes were very frequent, but have subsided considerably since and, were it not for the political agitation of certain radical elements, the number of wage disputes would be still smaller. Industrial arbitration courts established after the war have in many cases succeeded in bringing about industrial peace. In nearly all factories the workmen are represented by delegates in all negotiations with the employers.

Owing to the general European economic crisis, the industrial activity of Czechoslovakia, too, had to be considerably reduced. In the years 1921 and 1922 the activity in the various branches of industry was as follows:

Sugar production on the whole was highly satisfactory. Nearly 723,000 tons of sugar was produced in 1920-21 and 663,000 tons in 1921-22. Sugar is one of the chief export articles. The chemical industries suffered through lack of markets and their output amounted only to about 50 per cent of the prewar production.

Work in the building industries in 1921 was carried on to about one-fifth of the normal extent.

In the porcelain industry there was a great activity in the first two years following the war but since the rise of the Czechoslovak crown there has been a marked decline in the exports.

In the glass industry about 40,000 workmen are employed. The exports of glass and glassware in 1920 amounted to three billion Czechoslovak crowns, and held the second place in the exports. Of the total output of this industry 80 to 90 per cent is exported. The exports to the neighboring countries were greatly reduced owing to the currency conditions but the industry is finding new markets and is steadily improving the quality of its products.

The annual production of alcohol in the last four years amounted to 500 to 600 thousands hectoliters, representing about 30 per cent of the normal output. There are 965 agricultural distilleries and 60 industrial distilleries, yeast factories, and refineries.

Activity in the brewing industry was below normal on account of the decrease of both domestic consumption and exports.

Work in the leather industry was almost normal in 1921, but since then there has been a decrease mostly on account of the causes operating in all industries. The greater part of the output is consumed at home and the rest exported, chiefly to Poland, Hungary, Austria, Yugoslavia and Rumania.

Flour milling is carried on in more than 10,000 mills capable of grinding 17,300 tons of wheat or rye daily, *i.e.,* 5,250,000 tons annually. For the needs of the home population 2,700,000 tons of wheat or rye are required, while the home production amounts to 2,100,000 tons.

The prewar output of the paper industry was consumed at home to the extent of 75 per cent. However, as the majority of the factories of former Austria are now situated in Czechoslovak territory, the paper industry can export as much as 60 per cent of its output. The raw material for this industry is found at home. It is more difficult, however, to find foreign markets, for, as in the case of other industries, the main customers had been Poland and Hungary, and these countries are now suffering from the depreciation of their currencies, and are unable to buy.

The textile industry suffered immediately after the war from a shortage of raw materials. At present the supply of raw materials is normal, but, on the other hand, there are difficulties in finding foreign markets. Recent trade reports, however, indicate a noticeable improvement in this industry.

In the engineering and the iron industries there was a great activity during and after the war, but in 1921 stagnation set in. Of the twenty-seven blast furnaces in the territory of Czechoslovakia only eight are working at present. The engineering trades are well employed, large orders having been received from abroad.

Work in the coal mines was carried on below the prewar extent chiefly on account of the prevailing industrial crisis. Efforts to lower the cost of production and thus to reduce the price of coal have led to a general miners' strike which lasted seven weeks, from August 20th to October 6th, 1923. The strike has been settled by an agreement reducing the wage rates by 13 per cent. As a result of this agreement the price of coal has been reduced about 20 per cent.

In 1921 the unemployed in Czechoslovakia numbered 95,000 of whom 45,000 were supported by the Government. This was a great improvement over the year 1919, when approximately 267,000 were supported by the State. At the beginning of 1922, and especially in the second half of 1922, the number of the unemployed increased considerably, owing to the prevailing industrial crisis. In January, 1922, the unemployed numbered 113,015; in February, 142,454; in March, 128,336; in June, 107,702, and in August, 150,000. A year later, in August, 1923, the number of unemployed had declined to 61,438 and in September, 1923, to 57,000.

Social and industrial conditions in Slovakia were, on the establishment of the Republic, in a much more unsatisfactory state than in the Czech territories, for the Slovak workmen and Slovak industries were by no means so advanced as the Czech. There were many obstacles in the way of social and industrial consolidation, but in spite of them a marked progress has been made.

The same may be said of Carpathian Ruthenia, where economic and social conditions have also greatly improved. Carpathian Ruthenia has a great lumber industry and several important iron factories and agricultural distilleries.

The progress of the Czechoslovak Republic during the last five years may be briefly summarized as follows: The labor conditions in the industries have improved considerably in comparison with the conditions prevailing immediately after the war. The extreme radical elements have been routed and Utopian radical schemes have been abandoned excepting such really necessary social reforms as the old age pensions, social insurance, etc. Relations between employers and employees are friendly. With respect to the general industrial activity, it is expected that a general improvement in trade will take place as soon as the increase in the exchange value of the Czechoslovak crown has brought about a corresponding reduction in wages and prices. It will be possible then to settle the questions of taxation and the tariff, and thus to clear the political sky at home. The great mineral wealth of the Republic, the available water power, and the skill of the workmen must also be taken into account in considering the economic and industrial possibilities of the Czechoslovak Republic which is now gradually becoming a stronghold of order in the European chaos of political and economic anomalies.

CONTENTS

CONTENTS

CZECHOSLOVAKIA

I

POPULATION

DR. ANTONIN BOHÁČ, COUNCILLOR OF THE STATE BUREAU OF STATISTICS, PRAGUE

The Czechoslovak Republic came into existence on October 28, 1918, after the collapse of the Austro-Hungarian Empire. It was formed of territory which formerly belonged to three states: Austria, Hungary, and Germany. The Czech lands, Bohemia, Moravia, and Silesia, were formerly part of Austria. By the Treaty of St. Germain, Bohemia was given eleven Lower Austrian parishes and Moravia five. Slovakia and the autonomous territory of Carpathian Ruthenia (Podkarpatská Rus) were parts of the former Hungarian territories. By the Treaty of Versailles, Germany ceded a part of Prussian Silesia inhabited by Czechs, a district named Hlučínsko, which was united with Czechoslovak Silesia. Parts of eastern Silesia, the so-called Teschen, together with parts of the Orava and Spiš counties in Slovakia, were given to Poland.

1. AREA AND POPULATION

The Czechoslovak Republic has an area of 140,485 square kilometers (54,241 square miles) and, according to size, ranks fourteenth among the European states. The area is divided as follows: Bohemia, 52,052; Moravia, 22,304; Silesia (with Hlučínsko), 4,420; Slovakia, 49,015, and Ruthenia, 12,694 square kilometers.

According to the census of February 15, 1921, the Republic had a population of 13,613,172, distributed as follows:

Bohemia	6,670,582
Moravia	2,662,884
Silesia	672,268
Slovakia	3,000,870
Ruthenia	606,568

In population, Czechoslovakia ranks tenth among the European states; with respect to density it also holds tenth place.

The density of population in 1921 was 251 to the square mile. Czechoslovakia is one of the most thickly populated countries of Europe, but the population is not equally distributed. The Czech territories are more densely populated than Slovakia or Ruthenia, for in Silesia the population per square mile is 394, in Bohemia 332, in Moravia 309, whereas in Slovakia it is 159, and in Ruthenia only 124. The poor mountainous districts of central and eastern Slovakia, the northern mountainous part of Ruthenia and several unproductive counties of southern Bohemia and southwest Moravia are the least populous. Prague, the capital city, and its vicinity, several other large cities, and the coal district of Ostrava in Moravia and Silesia, with a population of 800 to 1,300 to the square mile, rank with the most densely populated regions of the world.

2. Growth of Population

Before the World War the annual increase of the population in the last four decades (outside of the period of the agricultural crisis in 1889-1890) was 7 to 8 per mille in Bohemia and Moravia, a little less (5 to 7 per mille) in Slovakia, and much larger in Silesia (10 to 12 per thousand); in Ruthenia the increase was very high (13 to 15 per thousand annually). In that period the Czechoslovak Republic occupied approximately the middle place between the European West and Southwest, where the increase of population was small, and Russia and the Balkans, where the population was rapidly increasing.

The population of Czechoslovakia was not increasing in all the districts at the same rate. The industrial and commercial cities were growing very rapidly, while the population of the poorer agricultural districts of southern Bohemia, southwestern Moravia, northern and eastern Slovakia and of the mountain districts of northeastern Bohemia and northern Moravia, where spinning and weaving were the chief home industry, was largely decreasing through emigration.

In the war Czechoslovakia, like all the other belligerent countries, suffered a heavy loss of population. From January 15, 1911, to January 15, 1921, the increase of population in its territory was only 13,972. In the largest territory, Bohemia, there was a decrease of 11,385, *i.e.,* 1.6 per thousand; but an increase of one per thousand was shown in Moravia and Ruthenia, and a slightly larger increase in Slovakia and Silesia (2 to 2.5 per mille). The largest decrease in population, according to the last census, occurred in those districts where large numbers of the population were employed in the textile industry which suffered from a shortage of raw materials during the war.

3. Marriages, Births and Deaths

Important changes were brought about by the World War. During the war and in the first years after the war the conditions were abnormal. In pre-war times, the natural movement of the population was as follows:

(*a*) *Marriages.*—In the years 1901-1910 there were, in the Czech territories, 79 marriages per thousand inhabitants; in Slovakia and Ruthenia the ratio was a little higher, approximately 83. The proportion of marriages to population in the Czechoslovak Republic was practically the same as in Germany and England.

(*b*) *Births.*—The birth rate in the Czechoslovak Republic was lowest in Bohemia, where, in the same period (1901-1910) there were 313 births (exclusive of stillbirths) per thousand inhabitants. The rate was much higher in Moravia (340) and in Silesia, and was highest in Slovakia and Ruthenia, where, during the ten years before the war, more than 400 births per thousand inhabitants were registered. The birth rate has decreased sharply in Bohemia, less so in Moravia and Silesia, while in Slovakia and Ruthenia the control of births is practiced but little.

(*c*) *The Death Rate.*—In the Czechoslovak Republic the death rate was much higher than in Western and Northern Europe. In the ten years 1901-1910 the death rate was: Bohemia 218, Moravia 230, Silesia

245, and Slovakia about 235 per thousand. The progress of medicine and hygiene has lowered the rate very noticeably.

Statistics relating to changes in the population during the war are available only for Bohemia, Moravia and the western part of Silesia; the data for Slovakia and Ruthenia have not as yet been collected.

BOHEMIA, MORAVIA, AND OPAVA

Year	Marriages	Births	Deaths	Excess of Births (+) or Deaths (—)
1911	74,497	276,453	198,643	+77,810
1912	73,262	267,965	196,041	+71,924
1913	69,574	262,892	183,070	+79,822
1914	58,552	257,265	181,981	+75,284
1915	37,188	188,657	193,900	— 6,243
1916	32,726	132,818	179,796	—46,978
1917	37,354	119,938	182,554	—62,616
1918	55,242	113,489	227,729	—114,240
1919	119,464	181,875	171,298	+10,577
1920	128,584	231,753	169,779	+61,974

In the above-named territories which had 9.74 million inhabitants in 1910, and 9.64 millions or a little more than two-thirds of the total population of the Czechoslovak Republic in 1921, there were 28.5 births and 20.5 deaths per 1,000 inhabitants in 1911. In 1920, when the natural changes in the population were not as profoundly affected by the results of the war as in previous years, there were 24.0 births and 17.6 deaths per 1,000 inhabitants.

The number of divorces in the Republic since 1919, when the new law regulating divorces came into effect, has been as follows: 1919, 2,015; 1920, 3,503; and 1921, 4,250.

4. Emigration

Before the World War, the territories of Bohemia, Moravia and Silesia lost by emigration approximately 27,000 inhabitants, and Slovakia about 30,000 inhabitants annually. From the Czech territories, more than one-half of the emigrants went to Vienna and other parts of Lower Austria, about one-third to the United States of America, and a small fraction to Germany. From Slovakia and Ruthenia the majority of the emigrants went to the United States, and only a small number found employment in Budapest or Vienna. After the establishment of the Czechoslovak Republic changes occurred in the migration. Many Czechoslovaks residing in foreign countries returned home, the attraction of Vienna and Budapest for Bohemian and Slovak emigrants was greatly lessened, and the new immigration law passed by the United States has undoubtedly had some influence on the migration to America. Sufficient statistical material is not available at this time to throw light on the intensity of emigration from the Czechoslovak Republic after the war.

5. Distribution by Sex, Age and Marital Condition

In the Czechoslovak Republic, as in all the countries of Central, Western and Northern Europe, there is an excess of women. Through losses of men's lives on the battlefields that excess has been intensified. The proportion of women is higher in the western part of the country than in the eastern; in Bohemia the number of females to 1000 males is 1080, in Moravia 1096, in Silesia 1079, but in Slovakia only 1056.

As a result of the war and the decrease of births there have been great changes in the proportion of the population according to age. In the whole Republic, excepting Ruthenia, for which data are not yet available, 399 persons in a thousand were below 20 years of age, 305 were 20 to 39, 202 were 40 to 59 and 94 were 60 years or over. The percentage of children and youths increases toward the East. In Bohemia 37.7 per cent of the population were below 20 years of age, in Moravia and Silesia 40.7 per cent, and in Slovakia 43.7 per cent. Conversely, there is a larger percentage of adults in the western part of the country than in the eastern part.

Of the total number of males in the country (exclusive of Ruthenia) in 1921, 578 per thousand were single, 384 married, 34 widowed, and 4 divorced; among the females, 523 per thousand were single, 363 married, 110 widowed, and 4 divorced. The war had greatly increased the number of widows, while the percentage of single persons was lowered by the decrease of births.

6. Race

A thousand years ago the whole territory of the Czechoslovak Republic was inhabited by Slavs speaking the Czechoslovak language. Only Ruthenia and the eastern districts of Slovakia were inhabited by Slavs speaking the Russian language, and on a narrow strip along the borders of eastern Silesia there lived Slavs speaking the Polish language. In those days the Czechoslovaks occupied a much larger territory extending far beyond the present borders of the Republic. In the South, the Czechoslovak territory extended down to the Danube, and even farther to a point where the Czechs had the ancestors of the present-day Yugoslavs for their neighbors; in the West the Czechoslovak territory extended far into Bavaria; in the North, into Prussian Silesia, where the Czechs came into contact with the Poles, and with the Lusatian Slavs of whom only a small group, the so-called Lusatian Serbs, have survived north of Bohemia in Saxon and Prussian Lusatia.

· An intermittent migration of the Germans from the West, and of the Magyars from the southern plains, into the territory of the present Czechoslovak Republic began early in the eleventh century. For several centuries the Germans have occupied the districts in northern and western Bohemia where Bohemia borders on Germany, and also a narrow strip along the southern border of Moravia, the northern section of Moravia and the southwest section of Silesia; they also founded several German enclaves in Czechoslovak speaking territory, not only in Bohemia and Moravia but also in Slovakia, in the Spiš districts in particular, where the Germans have been settled since the thirteenth century. The Magyars settled in a narrow strip of territory along the southern border of Ruthenia; they penetrated deeper into the country along the northern bank of the Danube toward the present city of Nitra. In Czechoslovakia, as in other countries of central and eastern Europe, many Jews have settled in the cities. Toward the end of the sixteenth century a number of villages were established on the borders of Czechoslovakia by exiles from Croatia, then menaced by the

Turks. In Ruthenia a few Rumanian villages have been founded.

According to the census of 1921, the distribution of the native population by race is as follows:

	Total	Per 1,000
Czechoslovaks	8,760,937	655.1
Russians (Great Russians and Ukrainians)	461,849	34.5
Poles	75,853	5.7
Germans	3,123,568	233.6
Magyars	745,431	55.7
Jews	180,855	13.5
Others	25,871	1.9

There were 238,808 foreigners in the country in 1921.

Bohemia and Moravia are inhabited only by Czechoslovaks and Germans. The Czechoslovaks have a majority of two-thirds in Bohemia and of four-fifths in Moravia. In Silesia the Czechs constitute almost one-half of the population (47.6 per cent), the Germans two-fifths (40.5 per cent) and the Poles one-ninth (11.2 per cent). In Slovakia more than two-thirds of the population are of the Czechoslovak race (68.1 per cent) and one-fifth Magyar (21.5 per cent). There is only a small minority of Germans (4.7 per cent) and Jews (2.4 per cent) in Slovakia. In Ruthenia the Russians make up nearly two-thirds of the population (62.2 per cent), the Magyars only one-sixth (17.0 per cent); in the cities there is a large minority of Jews (13.3 per cent).

7. Religion

The religious situation is somewhat complicated. After Bohemia had lost independence as a result of the Battle of the White Mountain (1620) the reigning Hapsburg family carried on a ruthless campaign of persecution against the Reformed Church in the Bohemian countries. Until 1781 no religion but the Roman Catholic was tolerated in Bohemia and Moravia; Jews were allowed to reside in cities but only in streets specially assigned to them. When the "Decree of Toleration" was issued (1781) a small fraction of the population (about 2 per cent) announced themselves to be of the Protestant faith. In Silesia the Protestants were permitted to maintain a church in Teschen, and eastern Silesia still has a large Protestant minority. In Slovakia the Protestants likewise enjoyed greater liberty, and many districts adhered to their faith; about one-sixth of the Slovak population has remained Protestant. The Russian population was, for the most part, of the Greek Catholic faith to which about 100,000 Czechoslovaks living in Eastern Slovakia also belonged. Shortly before the independence of Czechoslovakia was proclaimed about 60,000 Russians joined the Russian Orthodox Church. After the proclamation of Czechoslovakia's independence about 1.25 million people left the Catholic Church, of whom about one-half remained unaffiliated, two-fifths organized an independent Czechoslovak Church, and the remainder joined the evangelical churches. The number of Jews increases from West to East; in Bohemia they number only 1.2 per cent, in Slovakia 4.5 per cent, and in Ruthenia almost a whole sixth of the population is of the Jewish faith.

The distribution of the population by religion is shown in the following table:

Roman Catholics	10,384,833
Greek and Armenian Catholics	535,543
Protestants (all denominations).......	990,319
Czechoslovak Church	525,333
Russian Orthodox	73,097
Old Catholics	20,255
Jews	354,342
Other confessions	2,824
Unaffiliated	724,507
Unknown	2,119

8. Occupations

In Czechoslovakia the two main groups of occupations, agriculture and industry, are about equally represented. In Slovakia and Ruthenia agriculture is in preponderance, whereas in Bohemia the manufacturing industry, which began to flourish in the eighteenth century, now employs more people than agriculture. The distribution of the Czechoslovak population in Bohemia, Moravia, Silesia and Slovakia, by occupation, including both the persons actively engaged in the several occupations and the persons supported by them, is as follows:

	Bohemia	Moravia & Silesia	Slovakia	Total
Agriculture	1,989,368	1,176,122	1,818,895	4,975,085
Manufacturing industries and mining.	2,734,344	1,272,462	530,192	4,536,998
Commerce and transportation	833,695	343,992	230,624	1,408,311
Civil service, professions and the army	398,373	178,258	147,918	724,549
Other occupations..	723,802	364,318	273,541	1,361,661
Total	6,670,582	3,335,152	3,000,870	13,006,604

II

AGRICULTURE

Dr. Vladislav Brdlik, Professor at the Czech High Technical School, Prague

I. Production

(1). *Natural Conditions.*—The climate of Czechoslovakia is a mean between the moderate maritime climate and the extreme continental climate. The average precipitation is only 740 millimeters (in the mountains from 1,000 to 1,400 millimeters), while in France and Germany it is 710 millimeters, in England from 700 to 1,000 millimeters (in the mountains from 3,000 to 5,000 millimeters). However, two-thirds of the rainfall occurs in spring and summer. The favorable distribution of rain is due to the mountain ranges on the borders.

Condition of the Soil.—The greater part of the soil is heavy. In the low, most fertile parts of the country, beetroot, wheat, barley, rye and oats are cultivated. In the highlands, over 450 meters above the sea, the soil is still fertile enough for the cultivation of rye, oats and potatoes. In the highest parts of the country, above 650 meters, there are permanent pastures, but in some parts potatoes, oats, and even rye are also cultivated. In places where the soil is fertile and the climatic conditions favorable, special kinds of crops, such as hops, etc., are raised. When the condition of the soil in certain districts has been improved (an area of 1,800,000 hectares or about 30 per cent of the total arable land is to be improved) the value of the crops will probably be increased about 35 million dollars a year.

(2). *Economic Conditions.*—According to ownership, the land is divided as follows: of the total land (including the forests) 63 per cent is owned by farmers (holding up to 100 hectares), and 37 per cent by large estates (from 100 to 1,000 hectares) and latifundia (estates over 1,000 hectares). Of the total agricultural land (arable land, meadows and pastures), 80 per cent is held by farmers and 20 per cent by large estates and latifundia. The origin of the latter form of holdings is explained in the chapter on land reform. One-third of the arable land belonging to the large estates (in Bohemia 40 per cent, in Slovakia 25 per cent) is leased to small farmers.

Communications.—In former Austria there were 42 kilometers of roads to 100 square kilometers of land. In the territory of the Czechoslovak Republic, however, there were 60 kilometers of roads to 100 square kilometers of area. With regard to railroads, post offices and telegraph lines the position of the Czech territories before the war, in comparison with other states, was as follows:

	Railroads	Post Offices	Telegraph Lines
	(Per 1,000 square kilometers)		
	km.	number	km.
Great Britain	120	105	420
Germany	116	94	516
France	94	27	301
Czech territories	94	44	200
Italy	61	38	174

The elongated form of the Republic is rather a handicap to a proper distribution of production and consumption of agricultural produce, but, on the other hand, the agricultural industries are located in close proximity to the sources of the raw materials. Of the 400 million quintals of the annual harvest, about one-quarter is consumed by the nearest factories working up agricultural produce, about 60 per cent is used as fodder, 4 per cent as seeds, and 3 per cent consumed by the producers, so that only about 10 per cent is left for the market.

In Czechoslovakia there are 1.9 kilometers of waterways to 100 square kilometers of area (in Germany 3 kilometers). The proportion of waterways in Czechoslovakia will be increased considerably when the Elbe has been connected with the Danube by a canal via Přerov and Bratislava. Both the Elbe and the Danube will become important waterways connecting Czechoslovakia with the sea, benefiting not only the manufacturing industries but also agriculture.

Market Conditions.—Average prices (1909-1913) in prewar Austrian gold crowns (1 cr.=$0.203):

	1 metric ton of wheat	1 quintal of beef
Paris	255	153
Berlin	249	154
Prague	244	146
London	195	133

The following table shows, in crowns, the prices current in Czechoslovakia in the years 1913 to 1921 (the figures in bold type represent prices fixed by the Government):

	1913	1914	1915	1916	1917	1918	1919	1920	1921
1 ton of wheat ...	210	420	340	380	420	600	800	1800	3200
1 quintal of beef	162	185	370	618	633	620	729	2200	1650
Fertilizer (1 ton)	94	96	117	230	243	360	498	1920	1100
Fodder	168	185	320	620	470		1500	900	3200

Agricultural Population (Wages and working conditions).—Per cent of population engaged in gainful occupations:

	Professions, etc. (including the army)	Commerce	Mining & Industry	Agriculture & Forestry
Czechoslovakia	19.5	9.3	34.0	37.2
France	11.3	14.3	31.7	42.7
Great Britain	20.9	23.1	44.1	11.9
Germany	12.4	12.4	40.	35.2
Italy	8.7	7.4	24.5	59.4

Agriculture finds it more and more difficult to cope with the increasing demands of the growing industrial population of Czechoslovakia, for the percentage of agricultural laborers is decreasing. In the Czech territories, in 1890, 100 agricultural laborers had to supply the needs of 370 persons; in 1910, of 470 persons. The decrease of agricultural population is caused mainly by the exodus of agricultural laborers to towns, an exodus which has not been made good by the increase in the number of farmers.

In 1910, 100 agricultural laborers had to supply 1900 persons in Great Britain, 650 in Germany, 470 in Czechoslovakia, 440 in France, and 360 in Italy.

The men migrating from the country to the towns were, as a rule, the best workers, so that the shortage of agricultural laborers was felt all the more. The introduction of the eight-hour working day contributed to some extent also to the labor shortage on the land. The Czechoslovak farmers, however, are one of the hardest working, thriftiest and most progressive sections of the population.

Prewar annual wage of an agricultural laborer (in prewar Austrian crowns):

Czechoslovakia	610
Germany	640
Great Britain	1000

Great Britain, a country preeminently industrial, was able to pay much higher wages than other European countries.

State Support, Self-Help, and Tariff Protection.—In the Austro-Hungarian Empire protection played an important role in the development of economic conditions, yet, for a long time, the manufacturing industries alone were protected. Agriculture was not fully protected against foreign competition until 1906. Duties on cereals amounted approximately to one-fourth of the price. Protection was abandoned during and after the war, but in 1921 a tariff imposing a low *ad valorem* duty on the imports of cattle was introduced. The duties to be imposed on cereals are at present the subject of political negotiations.

The former Austrian Governments had no definite agricultural policy. Occasional subsidies were granted to the agrarians in return for political support, and that was about all. The great problems of the land reform, waterways, electrification, afforestation, and social reforms were studiously avoided. Czechoslovakia is now seeking a gradual solution of these important questions.

Cooperation.—The high standard of the Czech agriculture is due mainly to the voluntary cooperation of the farmers. The farming population has been organized by agricultural councils and corporations based on voluntary association of the interested producers and aided by State and provincial subsidies. These councils coordinated the labors of various agencies working for the improvement of agriculture and the promotion of agricultural interests. Their activity was hampered only by insufficient State grants.

Cooperative societies have grown up with the agricultural councils. Credit organizations, the first in the field, were established in nearly all villages. The farmers then proceeded to organize cooperative societies for the purchase of machinery, fertilizers and seeds, and for the sale of produce; cooperative warehouses, grist mills, distilleries, breweries, fruit-canning factories, building societies, etc. In Slovakia, however, cooperative societies worth mentioning did not exist; the societies shown in the Magyar statistics were but semiofficial consumers' societies and credit institutions. The organizing abilities of the Slovak farmers have been demonstrated only after the establishment of the Czechoslovak Republic, when, in the course of a single year, 969 cooperative societies were founded. Similarly also in Carpathian Ruthenia activities in this direction began only after the Magyar regime had been overthrown. At present there are about 10,000 cooperative societies in the country, with about one million members. Besides these a number of corporations for special purposes have been founded. In order to concentrate all the activities of the agricultural institutions, societies, etc., the Agricultural Union of the Czechoslovak Republic, a non-political central institution, has been organized.

In 1900 the Czech farmers established a political agrarian party for the protection and furtherance of agricultural interests which has become an important factor in Czech politics.

The Czech agricultural and forestry schools, too, owe their origin to the spirit of self-help of the Czech farmers. The only Czech college of agriculture maintained by the State was founded in 1906 as a special department of the Czech High Technical School in Prague. Since that time agriculture has been the subject of systematic study. The country now has 3 agricultural colleges with four year courses (1 German), 2 high schools of forestry and 1 veterinary high school, 12 agricultural secondary schools of which 4 are German, 4 secondary schools of forestry (1 German), 27 elementary agricultural schools (6 German, 1 Magyar), 96 winter courses (24 German, 1 Ruthenian), 9 special schools (2 German), 12 schools of horticulture (4 German), 4 elementary schools of forestry (2 German), 40 courses in domestic science (8 German, 1 Polish, and 327 popular agricultural schools (51 German, 15 Ruthenian), a total of 543 schools, or 1 school to each 240 square kilometers of area.

In former Austria the Czech territories had nearly two-thirds of all the schools with more than four-fifths of all the pupils. Under the Magyar régime there were no Slovak agricultural schools in Slovakia. It was only after the organization of the Czechoslovak

Republic that Slovak agricultural school were established. The number of popular courses in agriculture has been increased under the Republic from 45 to 327.

The education of the farmers was promoted also by more than 50 periodicals devoted to the technical and economic instruction of those engaged in agriculture, and by lectures and exhibitions. One general agricultural exhibition and twelve local exhibitions were held in 1922.

II. Agricultural Production

The general distribution of the area with respect to fertility is as follows (prewar data in percentages):

	Arable Land	Meadows & Pastures	Forests	Non-productive	Total in Hectares
Denmark	68	7	8	17	3,896,870
Czechoslovakia ..	45	18	33	4	14,048,500
Great Britain....	23	58	4	15	31,223,078
France	50	19	18	13	52,955,764
Germany	48	16	26	10	54,109,836

In Czechoslovakia, it will be observed, nearly half of the total area consists of arable land, and only 4 per cent is non-productive—a fact showing the intensity of Czechoslovak agriculture. In Czechoslovakia there is really no unused land, for the land classified in the above table as "non-productive" represents surfaces taken up by buildings, rivers, roads, etc. In Slovakia and Carpathian Ruthenia, however, it is still possible to increase the area of arable land.

The arable land is distributed as follows (per cent):

	Czecho-slovakia	Great Britain	France	Germany
Potatoes, vegetables	15	33	21	14
Beetroot, hops, other produce	12	21	9	16
Fodder crops	6	2	2	3
Fallow lands	7	..	11	7
Wheat	11	11	27	8
Barley	14	10	3	7
Rye	17	0.3	5	26
Oats	15	23	17	17
Corn (maize)	3	..	5	2

The production of beetroot, maize, wheat and barley shows the intensive cultivation in Czechoslovakia, while rye, oats and fodder indicate on the other hand its extensiveness. In Czechoslovakia, wheat and barley take up 25 per cent of the arable land, in Germany 15 per cent, in England 21 per cent, in France 30 per cent of the total arable land.

The Animal Industries.—The number of domestic animals per 100 hectares in various countries before the war is shown in the following table:

	Cattle	Swine	Sheep
Denmark	85	86	17
Germany	60	71	15.8
Czechoslovakia	51	29	15.7
Great Britain	42	13	82
France	34	18	44

The total weight of livestock in Czechoslovakia, amounting to 24 million quintals, was distributed as follows:

	Per cent
Cows	45
Other cattle	28
Horses	14
Swine	7
Sheep and goats	4
Poultry	2

Agricultural Industries.—The organization of agricultural production in the Czechoslovak Republic can not be fully understood without a consideration of its relation to the agricultural industries. There are in Czechoslovakia 189 sugar factories with a possible output of 1.7 million tons of sugar, 676 breweries producing 13 million hectolitres of beer, 1,110 distilleries producing 1,151,000 hectolitres of alcohol, 128 starch factories, 13 yeast factories producing 720 quintals, 140 malt factories producing 2,300,000 quintals of malt, 380 fruit-canning factories, 800 dairies (nearly 40 million hectolitres of milk are used for the making of dairy products), over 10,000 flour mills, and 40 factories making chicory and coffee substitutes with a yearly output of 600,000 quintals. These figures show the extent of the Czechoslovak agricultural industries. The extent to which the sugar and liquor industries have been developed is indicated in the following table showing the amount of sugar and alcohol produced to each 10 hectares of cultivated land in various countries:

	Sugar quintals	Alcohol hectolitres
Czechoslovakia	127	13
Germany	65	10
Denmark	46	7
France	20	5
Great Britain	9	4.7

There are in Czechoslovakia four main branches of agricultural activity: 1. sugar beet cultivation; 2. cereal cultivation; 3. cereals and potatoes; 4. pastures.

Fisheries.—The fish ponds cover an area of 45,000 hectares. These ponds are mostly situated in southern

Bohemia. The total length of rivers yielding fish is 19,000 kilometres. The annual catch of fish amounts in weight to 30,000 quintals and in value to about 50 million Czechoslovak crowns. Ninety per cent of the fish are carps and the rest are pikes, trout and perch. Before the war, the greater part of the catch was exported to Vienna and Saxony.

III

The relative position of the Czechoslovak Republic with respect to agricultural production is indicated in the following table showing the prewar annual yield of agricultural produce in various countries:

Annual Crop of Wheat, in Quintals

United States	186,889,000
France	86,447,000
Italy	49,876,000
Germany	41,400,000
Spain	35,502,000
Rumania	23,893,000
Great Britain	16,231,000
Czechoslovakia	9,825,756
Netherlands	1,333,000
Denmark	1,261,000

Production of Wheat Per Capita

Rumania	337.0 kg.
France	220.5 "
United States	202.5 "
Spain	178.0 "
Italy	143.7 "
Czechoslovakia	74.3 "
Germany	63.8 "
Denmark	45.5 "
Great Britain	35.7 "
Netherlands	22.6 "

Annual Crop of Rye, in Quintals

Germany	113,093,000
Czechoslovakia	15,735,819
France	12,453,000
United States	8,869,000
Spain	7,020,000
Denmark	4,824,000
Netherlands	4,109,000
Italy	1,354,000
Rumania	1,188,000
Great Britain	470,000

Production of Rye Per Capita

Germany	1.74 kg.
Denmark	1.74 "
Czechoslovakia	1.17 "
Netherlands	0.70 "
Spain	0.35 "
France	0.32 "
Rumania	0.17 "
United States	0.10 "
Italy	0.04 "
Great Britain	0.01 "

Annual Crop of Barley, in Quintals

United States	39,599,000
Germany	33,427,000
Spain	16,262,000
Czechoslovakia	14,899,289
Great Britain	14,226,000
France	10,491,000
Rumania	5,441,000
Denmark	5,352,000
Italy	2,200,000
Netherlands	710,000

Production of Barley Per Capita

Denmark	193.2 kg.
Czechoslovakia	114.0 "
Spain	81.7 "
Rumania	76.6 "
Germany	51.5 "

Production of Barley Per Capita—Continued

United States	42.9 "
Great Britain	31.3 "
France	26.8 "
Netherlands	12.0 "
Italy	6.3 "

Annual Crop of Oats, in Quintals

United States	164,190,000
Germany	85,929,000
France	51,569,000
Great Britain	29,986,000
Czechoslovakia	13,578,366
Denmark	7,558,000
Italy	5,363,000
Spain	4,225,000
Rumania	4,216,000
Netherlands	2,929,000

Production of Oats Per Capita

Denmark	272.8 kg.
United States	177.9 "
Germany	132.4 "
France	131.5 "
Czechoslovakia	102.9 "
Great Britain	66.0 "
Rumania	60.0 "
Netherlands	49.6 "
Spain	21.2 "
Italy	15.5 "

Annual Crop of Potatoes, in Quintals

Germany	457,758,900
France	131,985,900
United States	97,059,650
Great Britain	69,246,760
Czechoslovakia	64,743,229
Spain	27,456,230
Netherlands	23,833,850
Italy	16,548,880
Denmark	8,335,600
Rumania	1,238,170

Production of Potatoes Per Capita

Germany	7.05 kg.
Czechoslovakia	4.91 "
Denmark	4.04 "
France	3.37 "
Netherlands	3.01 "
England	1.53 "
Spain	1.38 "
United States	1.05 "
Italy	0.48 "
Rumania	0.17 "

Number of Cattle

United States (1913)	56,527,000
Germany	20,994,344
France (1912)	14,705,900
Great Britain	10,649,569
Italy (1908)	6,198,961
Czechoslovakia	4,607,341
Rumania (1900)	2,588,526
Spain	2,561,894
Denmark	2,462,862
Netherlands	2,096,599

Number of Cattle per 1,000 Inhabitants

Denmark	889
United States	612
France	375
Rumania	369
Netherlands	355
Czechoslovakia	339
Germany	323
Great Britain	234
Italy	164
Spain	130

Number of Swine

United States	61,178,000
Germany	25,659,140
France	6,903,750
Great Britain	3,162,462

Number of Swine—Continued

Czechoslovakia	2,580,086
Italy	2,507,798
Denmark	2,491,661
Spain	2,472,416
Rumania	1,709,205
Netherlands	1,350,204

Number of Swine per 1,000 Inhabitants

Denmark	899
United States	622
Germany	396
Rumania	244
Netherlands	228
Czechoslovakia	190
France	177
Spain	125
Great Britain	70
Italy	66

Annual Production of Sugar, in Quintals

Germany	22,898,504
Czechoslovakia	11,457,749
France	7,309,030
United States	6,291,791
Netherlands	2,287,732
Italy	1,893,089
Denmark	1,331,839
Spain	1,134,139
Rumania	367,524

Production of Sugar per 10 Inhabitants

Czechoslovakia	8.43	quintals
Denmark	4.61	"
Netherlands	3.88	"
Germany	3.53	"
France	1.87	"
United States	0.68	"
Spain	0.57	"
Italy	0.55	"
Rumania	0.52	"

Annual Production of Beer

	Hectolitres
Great Britain	56,000,000
France	15,000,000
Czechoslovakia	13,307,322
Denmark	2,600,000
Netherlands	1,800,000
Italy	500,000
Spain	380,000
Rumania	300,000

Production of Beer Per Capita

	Hectolitres
Great Britain	124
Czechoslovakia	97.9
Germany	96.1
Denmark	94
France	39
Netherlands	30
Rumania	4
Spain	2
Italy	1.5

Annual Production of Alcohol

	Hectolitres
Germany	3,632,684
France	2,699,400
Great Britain	1,192,643
Czechoslovakia	1,162,291
Netherlands	360,136
Denmark	145,900

Production of Alcohol Per Capita

	Hectolitres
Czechoslovakia	8.55
France	6.97
Netherlands	6.10
Germany	5.60
Denmark	5.27
Great Britain	2.63

It will be observed that with respect to agricultural production, the Czechoslovak Republic may be classed with the large States. It supplies the world market with 7 per cent of the total world production of sugar and with 15 per cent of the total beet sugar production.

The agricultural wealth of Czechoslovakia is clearly shown in a comparison of the annual production per head of population in the various countries. It will be seen that the Republic occupies an important place in the agricultural production of the world. Through the incorporation of agricultural Slovakia the Czechoslovak Republic has become nearly self-supporting as regards the supply of agricultural produce.

Of the total population of Austria-Hungary, 26 per cent are now in Czechoslovakia. While in the former monarchy there were 76 inhabitants to the square kilometre, in Czechoslovakia there are 97. In spite of the greater density of Czechoslovakia's population, however, the conditions of supply are by no means worse than they were in the former monarchy, as can be seen from the following table:

(Proportion per 100 inhabitants.)

	Czechoslovakia	Austria-Hungary
Potatoes, quintals	488	351
Sugar, quintals	84	30
Cattle, head	34	35
Swine, head	19	28
Alcohol, hectoliters	8.4	5.6
Beer, hectoliters	97	49

The value of the total agricultural production in Czechoslovakia estimated according to prewar conditions, amounts to 2,605,000,000 gold crowns, the value of the annual forest yield to 280 million gold crowns. The value of agricultural production, compared with other branches of production, is shown in the following table:

	Value of annual production (in gold crowns)
Agriculture	2,605,000,000
Mining	340,000,000
Sugar	120,000,000
Beer	170,000,000
Forestry	280,000,000

The total value of the agricultural production amounting to 2,605,000,000 gold crowns was distributed as follows:

	Million gold crowns or	Per Cent
Cereals	884	34
Potatoes	104	4
Sugar beet and chicory	173	6.6
Hops, tobacco, fruit, etc.	175	6.7
Beef	350	13.4
Milk, butter, cheese	445	17
Pork	282	11
Poultry and eggs	176	6.7
Mutton	16	0.6

It will be observed that the production of milk, butter and cheese exceeds in value the annual output of the coal and iron mines, and the poultry and egg production exceeds in value the annual output of each, the brewing and the sugar industries.

The national wealth as represented by agriculture is estimated, according to prewar statistics, at 25,092,067,000 gold crowns. Of this sum the value of the land represents 62 per cent, fruit trees 1.3 per cent, buildings 20 per cent, livestock 9 per cent, machinery 4.6 per cent, circulating capital 3.1 per cent. The forest wealth is estimated according to prewar statistics at 8,000,000,000 gold crowns of which the value of wood represents 81.8 per cent and the soil 18.2 per cent. The value of the sugar industry is estimated at 500,000,000 gold crowns and the brewing industry at 300,000,000 gold crowns. Of the total estimated value of agriculture, four-fifths are represented by land, buildings and trees, and only one-fifth is represented by working capital. The land alone represents nearly two-thirds of the agricultural wealth.

Agriculture and the War.—The decrease in agricultural production during and after the war was caused mainly by various results of the war, such as the shortage of labor, the general exhaustion, excessive slaughter of cattle, etc. Immediately after the outbreak of the war the shortage of labor became acute; there was a shortage of fertilizers, and the number of cattle was reduced 40 per cent. All this contributed to the decrease in agricultural production which, in 1919, was reduced to 60 per cent of the prewar average. This reduction expressed in value is estimated at 23 billion Czechoslovak crowns. The unsatisfactory postwar condition of agricultural production was reflected also in the Czechoslovak foreign trade which, in the first two years following the war, showed an excess of imports which depressed the exchange value of the Czechoslovak crown. After the war, agricultural production was also hampered by the arbitrary prices established by the State for agricultural produce whereby a great disparity was created between the domestic and the world prices. Thus, for instance, the farmer had to buy fertilizers abroad at current world prices, but for his produce he was paid for in prices fixed by the State, which were considerably below the world prices. Before the war, the farmer could buy 1 quintal of saltpeter for 1.2 quintals of wheat, in 1920 he had to pay 10 quintals of wheat. However, in 1921, when the agricultural production had reached the normal level, the State control of prices was abolished. It had been in force seven years. With the increased agricultural production the imports of cereals have been much lower since 1921.

The relation of the agricultural production to the foreign trade of Czechoslovakia is indicated in the following table showing the consumption and the surplus or shortage of the principal agricultural products (in millions of Czechoslovak crowns, according to prices current in 1922):

	Consumption	Surplus (for export)	Shortage (to be covered by imports)
Wheat and rye	5,809	....	518
Barley	1,148	1,026	....
Oats	1,484	672	....
Potatoes	1,054	248	....
Hops	40	47	....
Fruits	800	300	....
Meat	6,390	....	750
Fats	1,404	....	516
Sugar	637	1,550	....
Alcohol	734	482	....
Beer	1,980	414	....
Wood	1,184	416	....
		5,155	1,784

It will be observed that the total surplus of agricultural produce amounts to 5,155 million Czechoslovak crowns, and the imports to 1,784 crowns. The imports of fertilizers and fodder amount to 910 million crowns and the total imports to 2,694 million crowns, so that the agricultural production shows a surplus of 2,461 million crowns.

In weight the differences between production, consumption, surplus and shortage of the principal agricultural products, with a normal agricultural production, are as follows:

(In millions)

	Normal prouction	Consumption	Surplus	Shortage
Wheat and rye, quintals...	26.00	31.40	....	5.40
Barley, quintals	15.50	9.00	6.50	....
Oats, quintals	14.00	10.60	3.40	....
Potatoes, quintals	66.75	59.40	7.35	....
Hops, kilograms	9.60	4.40	5.20	....
Fruits, quintals	11.00	8.00	3.00	....
Meat, quintals	4.26	4.76	....	0.50
Fats, quintals	1.17	1.60	....	0.43
Sugar, quintals	11.46	3.30	8.16	....
Alcohol, hectoliters	1.16	0.70	0.46	....
Beer, hectoliters	13.30	11.00	2.30	....
Wood, cubic meters.......	16.00	11.84	4.16	....

The facts and figures quoted show the importance of agriculture for the economic life of Czechoslovakia. It is certain that with a sound economic policy and with the aid of the schools Czechoslovak agriculture will make further progress.

III

FORESTRY

Dr. Karel Šiman, Councillor of the Ministry of Agriculture

The forests covering about one-third (33.16 per cent) of the total area of the country are a very important part of the natural wealth of the Czechoslovak Republic and an essential asset of its economic life. According to the official statistics for 1920, altogether about 4,661,133 hectares are covered with forests and woods. Thus Czechoslovakia has a forest area comparable to that of Finland, Sweden, Yugoslavia, or Austria, four of the most thickly wooded countries of Europe. The plan for a gradual afforestation of denuded or unproductive land will add an area of 400,000 hectares, so that in the near future the afforested area will exceed 5,000,000 hectares. Thus Czechoslovakia, a comparatively small country, has a forest area nearly four times larger than that of the United Kingdom, one million hectares larger than that of Italy, or over one half of that of France. The most richly afforested part of the Republic is the eastern part; Ruthenia with 635,367 hectares (50.05 per cent), Slovakia 1,658,635 hectares (33.84 per cent), and Silesia 154,324 hectares (34.91 per cent). The western agricultural provinces of the Republic which are also highly industrialized show smaller afforestation:

Bohemia 1,569,965 hectares (30.16 per cent) and Moravia 642,842 hectares (28.82 per cent). The extent of the forests alone, however, does not give a true idea of the Czechoslovak Republic's wealth in wood. The best basis of estimate is the productiveness of the forests and the quality of the timber.

As to formation, high forests prevail and cover an area of 4,001,908 hectares (91.67 per cent); they are cultivated for a long period of growth according to the kind of timber: 80 years (Pinus silvestris), 90-100 years (Picea excelsa, Abies pectinata), 100 or more years (Fagus silvatica, Quercus). Low forests of soft timber (Alnus, Populus, Salix), or deciduous trees with hard timber (Quercus, Carpinus, Robinia), have an area of 295,397 hectares (6.30 per cent). The forests of medium height are situated chiefly in the plains along the Morava and the Dyje rivers in Moravia and along the river Labe (Elbe) in Bohemia as well as in Slovakia where they contain species of several genera of valuable trees (Quercus, Ulmus, Fraxinus, Acer, Betula) and occupy an area of 68,199 hectares (1.46 per cent).

Pure forests of coniferous trees cover an area of 2,148,548 hectares (53.68 per cent). Forests of deciduous trees extend over an area of 1,206,881 hectares (30.16 per cent), and the mixed forests of conifers and deciduous trees have an area of 646,479 hectares (16.16 per cent). In the western provinces of the Republic (Bohemia, Moravia and Silesia) the chief timber trees are the pine and the spruce (Picea excelsa, Pinus silvestris), in mixed forests of conifers the silver fir (Abies pectinata) and the larch (Larix europea).

Forests of deciduous trees (9.1 per cent) are composed mostly of beech (Fagus silvatica) and oak (Quercus pedunculata and sessiliflora) mingled with ash (Fraxinus), sycamore (Acer pseudoplatanus), Norway maple (Acer platanoides), elm (Ulmus montana, campestris) lime (Tilia), hornbeam (Carpinus), alder (Alnus), poplar (Populus alba, nigra), aspen (Populus tremula) and willow (Salix). The mixed forests of conifers and deciduous trees contain, beside the above named species, also the birch (Betula) and various kinds of the service-tree (Sorbus).

In the eastern sections of the Republic, in Slovakia and Ruthenia, the beech forests (Fagus) take up 42 per cent), the spruce forests (chiefly Picea abies) 33 per cent, and the oak woods on the southern plains 25 per cent of the woodland.

Recently various foreign trees have been introduced and proved successful, namely Pseudotsuga Douglasii (viridis and glauca) and Pinus strobus, also Picea pungens sitchensis, Abies concolor, Larix leptolepis: of the deciduous trees, Robinia pseudoacacia (especially adapted for the sandy soil of Southern Slovakia), Quercus rubra and in some places even Juglans nigra, Fraxinus americana.

It is also interesting to note the methods of administration and the productiveness of the forests. Out of a total afforested area of 4,661,133 hectares systematic management has been applied to 3,490,829 hectares (74.9 per cent), the wooded tracts being treated on a working plan carefully based on the expected yield. The area outside such systematic management is 1,170,304 hectares (25.1 per cent). With regard to the accessibility of the forests a regular exploitation is possible in the majority of the forests (4,001,906 hectares, 88.1 per cent). In Bohemia, Moravia and Silesia only 1,314 hectares of forests are excluded from the systematic management. These forests are on the high mountain sides and are maintained intact in order to protect the frontiers. In Slovakia and especially in Ruthenia there are still 477,025 hectares of forests not yet adapted for regular exploitation; in some cases these are primeval forests, and some forests in the mountains are not yet accessible.

The Government is now preparing a bill for the systematic management of all accessible forests based on definite plans of forest economy which will be subject to official examination and approval. These plans must be based on the principle that the annual cut shall not exceed the annual growth so as to insure a continuous and regular productiveness of the forests.

In the different parts of the Czechoslovak Republic the annual growth shows substantial variations due not only to the proportion of the various kinds of forests (high, medium and low), but also to the quality of the soil as well as the prevailing kinds of wood and the methods of forest management.

The annual growth per hectare of afforested area is 3.5 cubic meters; in the high forests it varies between 3.3 cubic meters (in Ruthenia) and 5.3 cubic meters (in Silesia), 3.4 cubic meters (Bohemia), 3.5 cubic meters (Slovakia), 4.2 cubic meters (Moravia); in the low forests the average is 2.5 cubic meters and in the forests of middle height the average is 3.0 cubic meters.

Taking the annual growth per hectare as the standard, we find that the total annual growth and therefore also the normal annual yield is as follows:

	FORESTS. High	Low (In cubic	Medium meters.)	Total
Bohemia	4,959,233	86,832	64,802	5,110,867
Moravia	2,132,420	74,580	118,001	2,425,001
Silesia	745,328	11,735	4,508	761,571
Slovakia	4,559,410	491,912	52,058	5,103,380
Ruthenia	1,860,220	10,666	1,254	1,872,140
	14,256,611	775,725	240,623	15,272,959

Furthermore when we consider that in Ruthenia and in Slovakia there are almost half a million hectares of old forests not yet opened to regular exploitation, we may estimate that Czechoslovakia will be able to produce in the near future, without endangering the normal yield, approximately 16 million cubic meters of wood because with the inauguration of rational methods of management in all the forests the annual yield will increase.

With regard to the annual yield of wood suitable for industrial and building purposes and of firewood, the official statistics for 1920 supply the following figures: 7,871,524 cubic meters (51.5 per cent) of wood for industrial and building purposes and 7,401,435 cubic meters (48.5 per cent) of firewood. However, as these figures were obtained in 1920, they can hardly be taken as normal, for the year 1920 was still a period of abnormal afterwar conditions, when the lack of coal made necessary the use of large quantities of first-quality wood as fuel. It is estimated that in the near future the yield of wood from those Czech forests where pine trees prevail will be increased 70 per cent (to 5,800,000 cubic meters); in Slovakia and Ruthenia, where large areas are covered with forests of deciduous trees (beech) not yet systematically administered, the yield will be about 9,300,000 cubic meters of wood suitable for industrial and construction purposes, and about 6,000,000 cubic meters of firewood. This yield, however, may be increased by the afforestation of numerous clearings and rational management.

The large forest wealth of the Czechoslovak Republic naturally has given rise to various industries. Timber and lumber are partly consumed at home and partly exported.

The annual consumption of quality timber, according to the statistics of 1920, is as follows:

	Cubic meters	Cubic meters
Normal yield		9,300,000
Pulp and paper mills	1,000,000	
Mining concerns	720,000	
Railroads (R.R. ties)	300,000	
Sawmills	6,500,000	
Telegraph poles, etc.	300,000	
Total home consumptions		8,800,000
Surplus for export		500,000

Wood is exported chiefly from Slovakia and Ruthenia. It is shipped by rail to Hungary or by the navigable rivers (Vah, Hron) to the Danube and by the Tisa to the East. Before the war, Bohemia exported large quantities of timber by the Labe (Elbe) river to Germany; at present, however, the exports are much smaller, owing to the expansion of the saw-mill industry which in most cases has its mills situated near navigable rivers. Consequently, large exports of timber from Bohemia can not be expected in the future.

The extensive saw-mill industry is capable of working about 6.5 million cubic meters of timber, from which about 3,900,000 cubic meters of sawed wood are made. This quantity of lumber is not all consumed in Czechoslovakia and a large part of it can be exported as semi-finished or finished products.

The total yield of firewood can not be consumed at home and a large part of it is exported, especially from Slovakia and Ruthenia, and what can not be exported is either burned in charcoal kilns or used in factories for dry distillation of wood.

Beside wood, the forests also yield tannin (from oak and pine) which is used in the leather industry, and forest seeds which the Czechoslovak woodlands yield in abundance, as well as different kinds of berries, mushrooms, peat, grasses, medicinal herbs, etc. The forest seeds are sorted in modern drying factories (in Lip. Hradok, České Budějovice, Brno, Trhanov Brandýs and Labem) and exported.

It is interesting to note the ownership of the woodlands in Czechoslovakia. In this respect we find a situation which substantially differs from the conditions prevailing in other European countries as regards State owned forests. Before the war, the Czech territories had practically no State owned forests (only 6,541 hectares), because the estates of the Czech crown had been sold by the Austrian Government. After the establishment of the Czechoslovak Republic, however, the State took possession of the estates of the former reigning family (76,924 hectares in the Czech territories and 33,229 hectares in Slovakia). In Slovakia the Government took over the former Hungarian State forests (199,630 hectares) and in Ruthenia 312,304 hectares, so that the State now owns 629,307 hectares (13.5 per cent) of the afforested area.

The following table shows the present forest holdings in the several provinces of the Republic:

Per Cent Owned By

	Total afforested area	State	Municipalities & Cos	Foundations	Church	Hereditary nobility	Other private owners
Bohemia, Moravia and Silesia....	2,367,131	3.38	10.61	1.34	7.92	24.96	51.79
Slovakia ...	1,658,635	12.9	24.2	2.7	4.6	10.8	44.8
Ruthenia ..	635,367	46.95	20.95	....	0.5	15.4	16.2

In a majority of the European countries the State owns a large proportion of afforested areas. When we consider that in Czechoslovakia the forests are largely owned by the nobility and other private owners we can understand why the Czechoslovak Government endeavors to enlarge its ownership of woodland to one-third of the total afforested area, as provided by the laws of the agrarian reform.

On the basis of the aforesaid principles the forest reform in Czechoslovakia seeks to improve the management of small forests owned privately or by the communes by transferring the ownership to forest associations. The safeguarding of forests against damage is an important task of the forest administration. Another task is the afforestation of waste lands and clearings for which the State is either organizing or subsidizing nurseries for the growing of sound trees. In this respect it may be mentioned that the State administration intends to promote the gathering of forest seeds from full grown and selected woods, and to exercise an efficient control over the selection of the seeds according to their origin, purity, and germinating capacity.

It is manifestly in the interest of the national administration of the forests and their gradual improvement that the people should be well informed about the importance of rational forest economy and the technical education of forest officials and employees who are in direct charge of the forest is no less important.

With these ends in view the State is carrying on an educational campaign among the population and planning a radical reform of the schools of forestry. The State has established forest academies, on the same high level as universities, in Prague and Brno, where forest directors and inspectors will be educated. High schools of forestry with four year terms have been established in Písek, Zákupy, Hranice, Ban. Stiavnice, where the forest administration officials will be educated, and also schools with one year terms for training of foresters (Domazlice, Jamnice, Lipt. Hajek). The State has also organized institutions of research (Prague, Brno, Báň. Stiavnice) which supplement the above mentioned schools. The county experiment stations are under the jurisdiction of the institutions for scientific research. By these measures it is intended to place the management of the forests on a scientific basis.

The success of the reforms which have been indicated briefly in this article will naturally be determined by the remedial legislation to be passed in the near future, and by the efficiency of the forest service under the national forest administration.

IV

LAND REFORM

Antonín Pavel, Secretary, Government Land Office, Prague

I. Reasons for the Land Reform

Czechoslovakia has been largely industrialized in the last two or three decades but still retains the character of an agricultural country. The social structure of Czechoslovak agriculture is, however, in a sharp contrast with the conditions prevailing in the manufacturing industries. The industries are modern while agriculture still bears the stamp of feudalism. A few hundred families hold enormous estates—latifundia—while the majority of the people own but small plots of ground or no land at all. There is no example of such unequal division of land in any other country of Central Europe.

The Distribution of Land Holdings.—In Bohemia seven-eighths of the population own no land whatever. Less than one one-hundredth (0.99 per cent) of the total area of the country is held by 373,088 owners owning little plots of one-half a hectare (1.2 acres) or less. The holders of farms varying in size from one-half a hectare to 5 hectares (1.2 to 12.3 acres) number 703,577 and their holdings represent only 13.39 per cent of the total area. In the class of estates of more than 100 hectares (247.1 acres) there are 1,548 holders possessing 37.63 per cent of the total area. Most of this land, however, is in the hands of 151 holders whose estates average between nine and ten thousand hectares (about 24,000 acres); their holdings aggregate 28.31 per cent of the area of the country. In other parts of the Republic the conditions are similar; in Slovakia and Ruthenia they are worse. These large estates, aside from the property of churches, monasteries, and foundations, have been protected in most cases by the law of entail.

Origin of the Latifundia.—The present division of land in Czechslovakia, socially so unjust, is not the result of a natural development of agriculture, but of a political and agrarian usurpation on the part of the Hapsburg dynasty in the seventeenth century. During the Hussite Reformation the property of the Catholic Church and a large part of the lands owned by the Crown had come into the hands of the nobility, who became energetic cultivators of the soil. In 1618 the Protestant nobility of Bohemia rose in defense of religious freedom. The revolt was crushed in the battle of the White Mountain in 1620, and Ferdinand II confiscated the property of all who had opposed him: the lords and the towns. The tragic results of the ruthless persecution of the Protestant population are described graphically by Ernest Denis, the French historian, in his work "Bohemia after the White Mountain." People of other faith than the Catholic were banished from the country and their property, if not retained by the Emperor himself, was granted away or sold for a song to his military or political favorites. In European history there is only one other such transfer of land on a large scale which might be compared to the confiscations of Ferdinand: the gradual expropriation of the holdings of the English earls and other large landowners by William the Conqueror after his victory on the hill of Senlac. In Bohemia the sale of such estates and the fines alone brought in 38,469,728 florins, an enormous sum of money at that time, the largest part of which came into the hands of the imperial court. Gradually a new nobility and new owners of latifundia came to power. They were mostly foreigners, as shown by their names: Liechtenstein, Trautmansdorf, Metternich, Aldringen, Clary, de Riva, Marradas, Bucquoy, Colloredo, Defours, Gallas, Piccolomini, Dietrichstein, Cerboni, Collalto, Huerta, etc.

The Habsburg usurpation of the land and the brutal persecutions estranged the Czech people forever from the dynasty and from the new nobility, who, from that time on until the downfall of Austria, were at once the champions and the tools of political, social and intellectual reaction. In the course of the seventeenth century the lands held by the new nobility were still further enlarged by the property abandoned by Czech exiles during the Thirty Years' War (1618-1648). The frequent rebellions of farmers in the seventeenth and the eighteenth centuries bear eloquent testimony to the desperate situation of the agrarian serfs, the real tillers of the soil in those times. The reforms introduced by Maria Theresa and Joseph II in the latter half of the eighteenth century brought about a certain improvement, but it was not until 1848 that the serfs were completely liberated. With the steady growth of population, however, the question of land reform became more pressing.

Emigration as a Result of Land Monopoly.—It is a well-known fact that districts with large landed estates lose a large proportion of their inhabitants by emigration, whether permanent or temporary. This social phenomenon has been observed in all European countries, and the Czechoslovak territories suffered large losses of population under the old Austrian régime. At present about 2,300,000 Czechoslovaks are living abroad, of whom approximately 1,200,000 are in the United States. According to the official statistics of Austria-Hungary, 197,373 emigrants left the Czech countries in 1891-1900, and 282,444 in 1907-1910. From the present territory of the Czechoslovak Republic 31,726 Czechoslovaks and Ruthenians migrated annually during the years 1910-1913 to the United States alone. The official figures would doubtless be much higher if they included the thousands of young men who without notice to the authorities fled from Austria to escape the military service.

This emigration, amounting to one-sixth of the Czechoslovak nation, can not be explained by land monopoly alone. In most cases, however, the land monopoly doubtless was the principal cause of emigration. Béla Kénez, the Magyar statistician, stated in an official publication issued shortly before the war by the Hungarian Bureau of Statistics, that 68 per cent of the emigrants from Slovakia were small farmers, farm workers, and day laborers. The number of emigrants, permanent and seasonal, increased almost automatically in the districts with many large and entailed estates, while in those regions where medium-sized and small farms predominated the number of emigrants decreased.

The emigration and its consequences, the loss of population, the flight to the cities, the decline in production and other economic evils can be combatted only by a destruction of the land monopoly, that is, by agrarian reform and an intensive internal colonization.

The Increasing Number of Tenants.—Another unhealthy consequence of land monopoly is the growing number of tenants, large and small. The existence of hereditary and inalienable large estates (entailed estates held by the nobility, the estates held by churches, monasteries, and foundations) and other large estates in the hands of a few scores of private landowners has given rise to a new social class, that of tenants. Some of these (wealthy individuals, sugar refiners, etc.) rent large tracts of land; some rent land to increase their own small holdings, while others own no land whatever. The conditions prevailing in the Czech territories are shown in the following table:

NUMBER OF AGRICULTURAL HOLDINGS ACCORDING TO THE LEGAL TITLE FOR THE USE OF LAND (1902 CENSUS)

		Total of freehold holdings	in %	Freehold and leasehold combined	in %	Leasehold	in %	Other forms of land holding	in %
Bohemia...	568,389	281,544	49.5	222.405	39.1	59,214	10.4	5,226	0.9
Moravia...	290,678	139,682	48.1	126.541	43.5	22.684	7.8	1.771	0.6
Silesia....	58,759	35,839	61.0	12.100	20.6	9.939	16.9	881	1.5

(Oesterr. Statistik LXXXIII.4)

In most cases rent is paid in money; in a few cases only the payment in money is combined with payment in kind. In Slovakia and Ruthenia, however, payment in farm produce is still customary. This kind of leasehold was already known to Aristotle and Plutarch; in ancient Rome it was called "colonia partioria." In southern and western Europe this form of leasehold is known as "metayage" or "métairie" and still predominates over other forms of leasehold; in Rumania it predominated until 1918. Under such a lease, which may be hereditary or only for a term of years, the tenant binds himself to turn over to the owner a part of his crops: one-sixth, one-fifth, one-fourth, one-third, one-half. The size of the owner's share in the lessee's crops is determined by the conditions of the lease, whether the lessee himself is to furnish seed, fertilizer, implements, and a team, or the lessor supplies a part of the equipment. In many cases the tenant, beside turning over a part of the crops, agrees to work for the lessor on certain days of the year. Since in the eastern districts of the Republic the large estates are all leased, the small farmers in Slovakia and Ruthenia are the victims of ruthless exploitation. It has been ascertained by Czechoslovak officials that through the payment in produce the lessor receives from a given tract of land a return six times larger than he would obtain in any other part of the country where rent is paid in money. The Czechoslovak Government has taken legal steps to facilitate a gradual commutation of this form of leasehold into leasehold paid in money. Only a thoroughgoing land reform, however, will put an end to the exploitation of the farmers in these districts where the old Magyar régime produced such unbearable conditions.

Economic Reasons.—The ambition of the great

landowner to enlarge his estate, to round it up by the purchase of the adjoining lands belonging to large or small farmers, usually made it impossible for the small landowner to extend his holdings. In the rare instances when land was offered for sale numerous buyers would bid up the price too high for the small farmer.

Statistics of the productive capacity of large estates in Central European countries of intensive production have shown that from the viewpoint of public welfare, only estates of not more than 250 hectares (618 acres) are economically justified, and that the number of the estates of that maximum size should bear a certain ratio to the number of medium and small holdings and that the latter should be in the majority.

The World War demonstrated the advantages possessed by a self-sustaining country. In Czechoslovakia the war sufferings have quickened the desire and the effort to make the country capable of producing a regular supply of food from its own resources. The land reform is regarded as a reliable means to increase agricultural production, especially with regard to meats, milk, eggs, fruits, vegetables, etc. The intensity of production on the large estates has its limits, particularly with regard to the quality of the produce. The production of bread grains in countries of extensive agriculture (Hungary, the Balkans, Russia) and the prospect that the grain of those countries will soon compete in the Czechoslovak markets compel the Czechoslovaks to apply new methods of production, as has been done in Germany, Denmark, the Netherlands, Belgium, and France, where intensive production prevails which depends on the predominance of medium-sized and smaller holdings over large estates. In Czechoslovakia the agriculturists as a class have suffered relatively small economic losses by the war. Owing to the high prices of farm produce, they have reduced their indebtedness, and in matters of capital and credit are now well equipped to perform the task which the land reform will impose upon them.

Social Reasons.—It cannot be overlooked that the socialist or communist movement which was so strong immediately after the war found numerous followers among the agricultural laborers on the large estates in Czechoslovakia. The knowledge that in all the countries of Central and Eastern Europe a land reform, if not a land revolution, was unavoidable gave a new strength to the yearning of thousands of small landowners, farm laborers and servants for a new adjustment of land ownership in their own liberated country. Some favor the reform program and others the socialist plan of cooperative ownership, but their chief object is one and the same: to abolish the land monopoly which has become unbearable on account of the great density of population, the demand for intensive production, and the impatience for a betterment of the social conditions.

II. The Leading Principles of the Land Reform

Attempts to settle the land question were made toward the end of the nineteenth and the beginning of the twentieth century in many European countries (Russia, 1882; England, 1887, 1892; Norway, 1903;

Denmark, 1904; Sweden, 1904; France, 1908; Spain, 1907; Germany, 1886, 1890, 1891, 1900, 1904, 1908). In Austria-Hungary nothing was done. Internal colonization was proposed in a bill introduced by Count Falkenburg in 1893, but the bill failed of passage. In Galicia a law was passed in 1906, but its results are not known. In the Czechoslovak territories nothing was done whatever. Consequently, when the monarchy was dismembered, and the independence of Czechoslovakia proclaimed (October 28, 1918) the land reform was one of the most important measures demanding the attention of the legislature. The necessary laws and regulations were adopted in the years 1919-1922. The leading principles of the land reform and some of its practical results can now be examined.

The Land Control Act.—The agrarian reform in Czechoslovakia is based on the Land Control Act of April 16, 1919. The purpose of the law is declared in section one in the following words: "In order that the conditions of land ownership may be adjusted, large landed estates situated within the territory of the Czechoslovak Republic, including large entailed estates, are hereby placed under Government control, and a Land Office is hereby created." Section two defines large landed estates as follows: "By large landed estates are to be understood such holdings of real property, with all the rights appertaining thereto, where the area within the territory of the Czechoslovak Republic, held by a sole owner or by the same joint owners, exceeds 150 hectares (370 acres) of farming land (fields, meadows, gardens, orchards, vineyards, hopyards) or 250 hectares (618 acres) of land in general. Husband and wife, not divorced, are to be considered as one person."

Here it may be mentioned that the terms of the law have been misunderstood in some foreign countries. The words "confiscation" and "expropriation" have been used in this connection, though the ideas represented by those terms are altogether foreign to the law. It is simply a control law—the land is laid under an embargo, and the owner's freedom to dispose of his holdings is restricted. This idea of restriction (la saisie, die Sperre) is new to Czechoslovak law; it is somewhat akin to the idea expressed in the classification of ownership in the old German law (Obereigentum, Nutzungseigentum). The law places the large estates under Government control so that the owner can no longer dispose of his land at pleasure. Without the consent of the Land Office he cannot sell, lease, mortgage, or subdivide his property. The restriction is in no way equivalent to expropriation. Government control does not deprive the owner of his right of possession; it merely restricts his freedom of disposal. The State reserves the right to examine into all proposed transactions in land and to decide, from the viewpoint of the agrarian reform, whether the action contemplated by the owner is compatible with the object of the reform and therefore to be permitted, or is prejudicial and therefore to be prohibited.

The law authorizes the Government to take over the land under its control and transfer it to new owners or tenants on payment of proper compensation to the original owner or owners of the land so expropriated. The special cases enumerated in the law where no compensation is to be paid have been modified by the Peace Treaties and by the Compensation Act. Under article 208 of the Treaty of St. Germain, compensation is to be paid even for the lands of the Habsburgs, the money to be remitted to the Reparation Commission.

Lands and buildings forming an independent legal and economic unit, not used in connection with farming on the expropriated land, are exempt from Government control. The property of the provinces, counties, and municipalities is likewise free from the restrictions of the law.

The law applies not only to large estates existing at the time of its promulgation but also to such large estates as may in the future be formed by the combination of parcels of land now free from restriction and control.

Persons engaged in the management of property under Government control, whether owners, tenants or others, are bound to manage it efficiently; otherwise the Land Office may remove them from the management, under the provisions of the law of February 12, 1920.

The right of the State to expropriate the large estates under its control is limited in one important respect. The owner may demand that a part of the estate, to be selected by himself, if practicable, not exceeding 150 hectares of arable land, or 250 hectares of land in general, shall be reserved for him. In special cases a larger area may be so reserved, though the reservation may not exceed 500 hectares (1,235 acres) in any case. In determining the size of the area to be reserved the Land Office is to consider the needs of the population, the fertility of the soil, the interests of the agricultural industries, of the cities to be supplied, and other interests of the public weal.

At the end of 1921 the area under control aggregated 3,945,784 hectares (9,750,206 acres) or 28.1 per cent of the total area, distributed as follows:

STATISTICS FOR LAND UNDER RESTRICTION

Category:	Total area in hectares	Area under in hectares	control per cent
Fields	5,892,834	997,128	16.9
Meadows	1,388,816	200,957	14.5
Gardens	145,705	22,490	15.4
Vineyards	17,422	1,431	8.2
Pastures	1,212,058	181,454	15.0
Forests	4,654,911	2,445,658	52.5
Lakes, marshes	78,886	40,606	51.5
Unproductive	647,878	58,059	9.0
	14,038,510	3,945,784	28.1

The table shows the area and the proportion of the land under control. From the figures given in the table it will, of course, be necessary to deduct the area (estimated at 281,550 hectares) which will be left in the possession of the original owners under section 11 of the Land Control Act, and the area which may be released from control by the Land Office. The remainder of the land under control will be disposed of in accordance with the agrarian reform laws.

Expropriation of the Large Estates and the Rate of Compensation.—These questions are regulated by the law of April 8, 1920, and the supplementary law of June 13, 1920. The principle of eminent domain, the right of the State or the people in their corporate capacity to take land or other private property for public benefit, is recognized by all nations possessing a constitutional government. The right of expropriation was recognized by article 365 of the Austrian Civil Code. Expropriation of private property for public uses is likewise authorized by the Constitution of Czechoslovakia. The agrarian reform is essential to the welfare of society, and the land to be distributed will be acquired by agreement with the owners or under the right of eminent domain. In the latter case the compensation to be paid for the land taken over will be determined on the basis of the average prices obtained in the years 1913-1915 at voluntary sales of tracts of land exceeding 100 hectares in area. The Government is expressly directed by the law to assess at a uniform rate the value of real property of the same category, quality and location. By the decree of January 21, 1920, the country has been divided into four distinct regions of production (sugar beets, cereals, cereals and potatoes, pastures), the lands within each region being classified according to their character (land with or without buildings, vineyards, forests, etc.). The average value of land per hectare is calculated on the basis of the average net income, which is multiplied by a coefficient varying with the special character of the land, its distance from a railroad station, and other factors affecting the value of land in general. The value thus ascertained may be increased or reduced according to the actual condition of the property. Under the decree of September 21, 1922, the assessed valuation may be increased not to exceed 5 per cent in the case of land without buildings; 10 per cent in the case of land with buildings, vineyards in Slovakia and Ruthenia, or forests; and 15 per cent in the case of buildings alone. The value of buildings occupied by agricultural or forest industries, such as breweries, distilleries, brick yards, grist mills, sawmills, etc., coming within the scope of the law, is to be estimated by experts on the spot. In the case of forests, the quality of the timber as well as the quality of the soil and the age and the quantity of the trees are to be taken into consideration.

In the expropriation of the latifundia or estates of more than 1,000 hectares (2,471 acres) the total compensation is to be reduced, as land always brings lower prices when sold in large tracts. Under an amendment to the law of 1922, 1 per cent is to be deducted for each 100 hectares in excess of 1,000, but the aggregate reduction may not exceed 40 per cent of the total assessed valuation.

When a larger part of the inventory is to be expropriated with the land such inventory is to be paid for in cash according to the current prices. Investments made since 1914 are valued separately according to the real returns they yield. Fruit-bearing trees and new crops, or investments in crops, are likewise listed separately.

The State naturally cannot pay the inflated war or postwar prices for the land expropriated. Owing to a shortage of foodstuffs in Central Europe the prices had risen enormously during the war; at the present, however, the prices of agricultural produce are lower, and the value of land has declined in proportion. In view of these changes the compensation paid in Czechoslovak currency, now happily stabilized, may be considered by an impartial critic as adequate. A comparison of the rates of compensation authorized by the land reform laws of Germany, Poland, Yugoslavia and Rumania with the rates established in Czechoslovakia will not be to the disadvantage of the latter.

The owner of land under control, feeling himself aggrieved by any administrative finding of the Land Office, may appeal to the Supreme Administrative Court for relief. In case he considers the assessed valuation too low he may appeal to the regular civil courts of the first instance, the appellate courts, and finally to the Supreme Court. The Land Office determines the amount to be paid but the final decision rests with the courts.

The Payment of Compensation.—The compensation for the property expropriated, when legally established, constitutes a claim of the original owner against the State, unless the amount has been exhausted by the satisfaction of the lawful claims of third parties (mortgage or judgment creditors, employees, etc.).

The State may pay the amount assessed as compensation in cash, and does so in some cases. It is evident, however, that an immediate payment of large amounts would require large funds and might lead to a sudden increase in the circulation of paper money and to monetary inflation. Payments in ready money would therefore tend to depreciate the currency to the disadvantage of both the State and the creditor.

The payment of compensation is regulated by the laws of April 8, 1920, and July 13, 1922. As a rule, where the Land Office does not decide on immediate payment, the amount of compensation is recorded in a register of indemnities and is regarded as a State debt. The debt bears interest at the rate of 4 per cent per annum, and the Government is bound to amortize at least one-half of one per cent of the debt annually. The register of indemnities is kept by an office known as the Indemnity Bank, and the bank may tender a payment of the debt, on three months' notice, either in ready money or in other obligations of like value and bearing the same rate of interest. The creditor cannot demand payment in advance but may sell or assign his claim if he so desires.

Debts secured by mortgage on the expropriated land are likewise entered on the register of indemnities. In some cases payment cannot be demanded within five years after registration. The pension claims of employees, which terminate with the death of the claimant, will be satisfied from the interest on the compensation recorded in the register of indemnities so far as such interest may suffice.

Allotment of Land.—The principles which are to govern the allotment of the expropriated lands to claimants are indicated in the Land Control Act and developed in detail in the law of January 30, 1920. The law provides that the State may retain the land for the purposes of public utility, or sell or lease it to small farmers, subtenants, small business men, landless persons, and particularly to legionaries or war invalids willing and able to farm the land, or to cooperative societies of such persons; to cooperative societies of home builders, consumers, or farmers; to communes or other municipal corporations for public purposes; or to scientific or charitable institutions.

The law seeks to enlarge the present petty holdings

into self-sustaining farms of at least 5 to 15 hectares (12 to 37 acres), the size depending on the fertility of the soil, and to establish new farms by internal colonization. It is not the aim of the reform to break up large estates into small and thus lower the standard of agricultural holdings. In the division of a large estate only so much land will be allotted to local applicants that the remainder, with the buildings, will form an independent economic unit. The large estate will still be an important factor in Czechoslovak agriculture when the reform has been carried out in its full extent, for private estates of 150 hectares and public estates of more than 150 hectares will be conserved. The lands of the large estates in excess of the statutory maximum are to be sold or leased to individuals or to associations when not retained by the State for public purposes. Among individuals the former owners or employees of the estate are to be preferred over other claimants. To make possible the acquisition of land in regions where no land is available for allotment, the law permits a voluntary exchange of free lands in such regions for land under control elsewhere. When the land is divided, farms consisting of isolated parcels are consolidated into one-tract farms wherever possible, by transfer or exchange.

Land under forests is not to be divided. The large forests will be taken over by the State, and the smaller tracts allotted to communes or counties. In Czechoslovakia the forest domain of the State, including the forests of the old monarchy acquired under the peace treaties, is comparatively small, representing only about 13 per cent of the total afforested area of the country, as against a proportion of about 30 per cent of State forests in other European countries.

The allotment law introduces the principle of family property into the agrarian organization of the Czechoslovak Republic. The property allotted under this law is designated as "an indivisible farm unit" (rolnicky nedíl) and may not be alienated or mortgaged without the consent of the Land Office. Such units are to measure 6 to 15 hectares.

In those cases where the taking over of large tracts of land and its distribution would require a long time the owner of property placed under Government control in 1920 or 1921 may be ordered to lease a part of the farming land to persons authorized by the law to apply for allotments (the so-called forced lease under section 63 of the Land Reform Law). Such leases may be ordered only in those cases where the proper administration of the large estate will not suffer thereby. The leases are made for six years.

Credit Assistance to Applicants for Land.—Some of the applicants for land are able to pay cash. Many others are not, though they may possess the necessary experience. The latter class includes a considerable proportion of the officials and employees of the large estates. As it would be a distinct loss to Czechoslovak agriculture if men of experience were to be deprived of the opportunity to become independent farmers, a system of farm credits has been established by the law of March 11, 1920, to enable claimants of limited means to purchase land. Under the law mortgage loans may be made to applicants in amounts not exceeding 90 per cent of the value of the land or 50 per cent of the value of buildings. Loans of higher amounts may be made to legionaries, disabled soldiers, or their dependents.

The credits are granted in various forms. When the State has taken possession of the land after crediting the original owner with the proper amount on the indemnity register, an account is opened in the indemnity bank for the applicant, the bank taking a mortgage as security. The State may become surety for the new tenant when he borrows money from the bank under favorable conditions for the purposes of improving the property by buildings or in other ways. The property thus mortgaged may not be alienated without the sanction of the Land Office until it has been cleared of incumbrances, nor within ten years in any case. The debtor is subject to the control of the authorities and may be dispossessed if he does not meet his obligations.

Applicants for land may also obtain short-term credits from the Land Office or from the banks on a guaranty by the Land Office. The Land Office grants credit only to cooperative societies borrowing for the account of a member or on their own behalf. In this connection the Land Office expects the applicants to use the services of the Raiffeisen and the Schultze-Delitzsch savings banks, which are to be found in nearly all Czech villages of any size. The aggregate liabilities of the State assumed in guaranteeing the loans is not to exceed 200 million crowns (about $6,000,000).

For the purposes of internal colonization a special fund of 20 million crowns has been established in the

Land Office by four annual appropriations of 5 million crowns. Various fees and fines are to be paid into this fund, including a fee of 10 per cent of the market price of the property released by the Land Office from control; 0.25 per cent of the rent paid under approved leases of property under control; 15 per cent of the fees payable on allotment and transfer, and all fines collected for violations of the land reform laws and regulations issued under the authority of those laws.

The Land Office and Its Duties.—The Land Office at Prague is a central bureau established to administer the land reform laws. Its duties have been defined by the law of June 11, 1919. The office is under the jurisdiction of the Council of Ministers. It is directed by a chief and two assistant chiefs. The chief or one of his assistants represents the Land Office before the Council of Ministers. Branch offices may be established in various parts of the country when necessary.

The Land Office is authorized to ascertain the area of land to be placed under Government control and to make such control known by entries on the registers of deeds; to release certain lands from control; to see that land under control but not yet taken over is worked properly; to issue permits for the sale, lease or pledge of land under control; to determine the amount of compensation to be paid for property taken over; to take possession of such land and sell or lease it to applicants properly qualified; to grant credits and other assistance to the new tenants; to encourage the organization of agricultural cooperative societies, etc.

The Land Office decides all questions arising under the land reform laws except such as have been reserved to the courts or other bureaus.

The officials of the Land Office include lawyers, engineers and agriculturists. The work of the Land Office is supervised by a governing board of twelve members elected by the Chamber of Deputies for three years. The Land Office submits reports of its work to the board at regular intervals, and the board may require special reports at any time. In a few cases when questions of special importance are under consideration the decisions of the Land Office have to be submitted to the board for approval.

III. Some Results of the Land Reform

Leaseholds Commuted Into Freeholds.—The law of May 27, 1919, authorized the county courts to convert leaseholds into freeholds under certain conditions. Application for such conversion could be made only by the lessee of a small farm held and cultivated by him or his family at least since October 1, 1901, provided the land rented by him was the property of the State, or under the control of the Government, or was a part of an estate registered in the land register of the Province, or of an estate owned by the Church or a foundation. The applicant had to prove that, with the acquisition of such land, his total holding of farming land would not exceed 8 hectares. He would then obtain a deed on payment of a compensation agreed on or determined by the court after a hearing of experts. Under this law 93,977 hectares (232,221 acres) of land had been purchased by the end of June,

1922, according to the official statistics of the Ministry of Justice.

Forced Leases of Land Under Control.—The Land Office had been organized September 15, 1919, but could not undertake the expropriation and distribution of land on a large scale until the principles governing the payment of compensation had been definitely established by the ordinance of February 16, 1921. In the meantime the demand for land was partly satisfied by leases of arable lands under Government control granted to applicants properly qualified for terms not exceeding six years. This action, taken at a time when the agrarian reform laws were in the course of preparation, contributed to the consolidation of the internal political conditions, for it was an earnest of the Government's intention to carry out the land reform. About 142,000 hectares of arable land was allotted under the "forced lease" provisions of the law.

Definite Allotments of Land, 1920-1922.—The Czechoslovak land reform is an undertaking of such a magnitude that it cannot be accomplished all at once. Nor is there any intention to do the work hurriedly, for the land laws have been conceived in an evolutionary, not revolutionary, spirit, and no sudden transformation of the agricultural and social structure is contemplated. The reform will be carried out gradually so that the experiences gained in the early stages of the work may be utilized and the economic and social effects of the reform studied. In 1920-1921 about 26,000 hectares of land were expropriated and allotted. In 1921 a working program for a period of three years was elaborated, and a list of the estates to be expropriated was published so that the owners and tenants would be informed in advance. In 1922 an area of 62,208.12 hectares was allotted for building purposes. In 1923 the State took possession of 244,000 hectares of forests located partly in the interior and partly along the borders. All employees of the original owners were taken into Government service.

The arable lands are taken over by the new owners only after the harvest. In Slovakia and Ruthenia the work of internal colonization has begun and several new villages have been founded. When the prices of building materials have declined and the costs of building operations have been reduced the work of colonization may be expected to proceed with greater rapidity.

Conclusion.—The legitimate interests of all property owners affected by the land reform are conserved and respected as long as they do not endanger the success of the work. Special care has been taken not to hamper the development of the various industries closely associated with agriculture (sugar, alcohol, etc.). The officials and employees of the large estates who have lost their positions by the expropriation of the estates are to be indemnified for the loss. Under section 75 of the Compensation Law they may receive an allotment of land, or another suitable employment, an indemnity in cash, or an invalid or old age pension.

It is not intended to carry out the land reform according to any cut and dried schedule, scheme or doctrine. The work is a continuous process of adjustment. In technical questions of importance the opinion and advice of experts is sought, and special consulting committees, both local and regional, have been established.

The results of the agrarian reform thus far achieved are highly satisfactory. No unfavorable influence of the reform on agricultural production has been observed but rather the contrary. Individual interest in farming has been intensified, for the ownership of land which had been but an aspiration and a pious wish to many is an inspiration to the new owners. The assistance of the numerous schools and colleges of agriculture is of special value to the new farmers. The agrarian reform will be carried out strictly on an evolutionary and constructive basis, without any economic or social upheavals, so that it may become one of the economic mainstays of the liberated country.

V

COAL

Dr. Joseph Peters, Director of the Czechoslovak Mine Owners' Association, and Lecturer on the Mining Law at the Charles University, Prague.

The coal resources of the Czechoslovak Republic consist of several coal fields and lignite basins, the largest of which are situated in northern Moravia and Silesia and northwestern Bohemia.

Bohemia's coal deposits are located near the northeastern border, in the neighborhood of Žacléř and Svatoňovice; in the territory northwest of Prague in the Kladno and Rakovnik districts; and in the southwestern part of Bohemia in the Plzeň district. There are also two small basins in the Budějovice district and on the northeastern border near Brandov. In Moravia and Silesia the largest and the most important field is that of Ostrava-Karvin, beside which there are small coal deposits at Rosice and Oslavany.

The most important and the richest coal field is that of Ostrava-Karvin which forms the southwestern extension of the large Moravian-Silesian-Polish basin which covers an area of about 6,920 square kilometers; of this area Czechoslovakia owns about 15.6 per cent. This basin, in which there are several large coal beds, may be estimated to contain from 4,733 to 6,144 million tons of workable coal within a depth of 1,200 meters. The coal is of the very best quality, having a heating value of 6,000 to 7,000 calories.

The Kladno-Rakovnik basin has one main seam 6 to 11 meters in thickness above which there is a thin vein chiefly in the vicinity of Slany. The coal from the main seam is of good quality and has a heating value of 5,000 to 5,700 calories.

The area of the Plzeň basin is about 450 square kilometers. The coal is of very good quality, rich in gases, and has a heating value up to 7,000 calories.

The Zacler-Svatonovice basin forms a part of the Lower Silesian Waldenburg basin; the extent of this field in the southeast direction has not as yet been ascertained. In this basin there are about 28 seams of varying thickness and quality of coal. In the Rosice-Oslavany basin, west of Brno, there are three veins, which are only partially accessible. The coal has a heating value of 6,000 to 7,000 calories and contains a large quantity of sulphur (2.68 to 3.75 per cent).

In Slovakia deposits of lignite are found in several places. Small beds of lignite are worked also in the Kyjov district in southern Moravia. The chief sources of lignite are, however, the three basins in northwestern Bohemia along the Ore Mountains, from Cheb (Eger) to the right bank of the Labe (Elbe). These are known as the Most-Chomutov-Teplice basin, the Falknov-Loket-Karlovy Vary basin, and the Cheb basin, these three belonging to the late Oligocene and the lower Miocene series.

The most important of these three fields is the Most-Chomutov-Teplice basin between Kadaň and Ceská Kamenice. The quality of the coal varies according to location; the deeper the deposits, the better the quality of the coal; the heating value varies from 3,000 to 7,000 calories.

In the Falknov-Loket-Karlovy Vary basin there are several seams which contain lignite of very good quality, rich in gases. Very good gas coal is found in the middle depoits of the "Anezka" mine; the coal from the uppermost vein of the "Antonin" is less good.

In the Cheb basin lignite is found in seams about 30 meters in thickness. This coal has a heating value of about 4,000 calories and contains much water. It is well suited for the manufacture of briquettes.

The total output in 1921 was 11.65 million tons of coal and 21.05 million tons of lignite. The industry gave employment to 127,329 workingmen, of whom 75,906 were mining coal and 51,423 lignite. Before the war, in 1913, the coal mines located in the territory now belonging to the Czechoslovak Republic yielded 14.27 million tons of coal and 23.11 million tons of lignite, and employed 97,791 workmen. The decrease in the output, as compared with prewar production, amounts to 18.4 per cent in the case of coal and 8.9 per cent in the case of lignite. In 1922, owing to the general industrial crisis which hampered the exploitation of the mines, the output increased but little.

The following table shows the output and the number of workmen employed in the various basins in the years 1913 and 1921:

(a) COAL

Mining area:	1913 Output in thousands of metric tons	1913 No. of workmen	1921 Output in thousands of metric tons	1921 No. of workmen
Praha	510	2,501	433	3,904
Slaný	2,033	8,963	1,740	10,322
Plzeň	1,362	7,175	918	7,286
Kutná Hora	462	2,532	424	3,640
Most-Chomutov	35	143	25	258
Brno	506	2,743	345	3,438
Mor. Ostrav	9,363	38,493	7,763	47,058
Total	14,271	62,550	11,648	75,906

(b) LIGNITE

Mining area:	1913 Output in thousands of metric tons.	1913 No. of workmen.	1921 Output in thousands of metric tons.	1921 No. of workmen.
Most	13,926	19,621	10,514	23,702
Teplice	2,733	5,058	3,115	7,782
Chomutov	1,948	2,471	2,459	5,632
Karl. Vary	4,097	7,095	4,516	11,295
Ces. Budéjovice	4	86	1	4
Slaný	..	..	1	6
Kutná Hora	53	93	44	86
Brno	255	621	181	807
Mor. Ostrava	1	3	2	4
Slovakia	96	190	219	2,105
Total	23,113	35,241	21,051	51,423

The quantity of coal consumed in the Czechoslovak Republic in normal times cannot as yet be ascertained as the prewar statistics relate to the whole Austrian empire and not the individual territories. On the basis of the available sources of information it may be estimated that the per capita consumption is approximately 2 tons of lignite. On this basis of calculation the total consumption would amount from 26 to 30 million tons of lignite or from 15 to 18 million tons of coal (in the proportion 1:1.7).

It is evident that the output of coal in the Czechoslovak Republic exceeds the home consumption, and consequently it is possible to export a considerable quantity of coal. The exports of coal from the Czechoslovak Republic are not the result of the surplus of production only, but are also due to the geographical location of the coal basins and the quality of the coal.

The largest coal basin, Ostrava-Karvin, is situated near the borders of Poland and Germany, in the vicinity of the great coal basin of Upper Silesia which has always been the chief competitor of the Ostrava coal. The Ostrava coal is best suited for coking, for it is rich in gases and thus surpasses the Upper Silesian coal in quality, but, because of its adhesive character it is less popular as either household or industrial fuel than the Upper Silesian coal. Prior to the war the administration of the Ostrava-Karvin basin would turn most of the coal into coke for which there was a large demand both at home and abroad. Thus the Ostrava-Karvin basin depends on exports even though it is more favorably situated as to the nearest markets in Moravia and Slovakia than the Upper Silesian basin.

The competition of the Upper Silesian coal with the Ostrava coal was detrimental to the latter, even in the nearest natural markets because the Upper Silesian coal had more favorable geographical conditions and could be sold at a lower price because of the large size of the strata. The exports from Ostrava were directed chiefly to the South, to Austria and Hungary, and also to Poland and Russia.

The production of coke in the Ostrava-Karvin district since 1910 is shown in the following table:

Year	Production of coke (in thousands of metric tons)
1910	1,934
1911	2,002
1912	2,248
1913	2,507
1914	2,124
1914	2,124
1915	1,890
1916	2,509
1917	2,544
1918	2,071
1919	1,576
1920	1,663
1921	1,385

The other coal basins depended on the home market in the majority of cases; only a part of the output of the Plzeň and the Kladno basins was exported, chiefly to Bavaria.

The Czech lignite basins regularly exported a large part of the output; their natural markets were over the western borders of the State, in Germany. As regards the Most-Teplice-Cheb basin, it was the cheap transportation by the river Labe (Elbe) connecting the basin with the more important markets in Saxony that played an important part in the development of the basin. The exports by way of the Labe are important especially during the summer months when the consumption of coal at home is slack.

The exports to Germany are one of the conditions

of the development of the lignite basins of northern Bohemia, and a vital necessity for the Falknov-Loket basin. The sale of the Falknov coal, as far as home consumption is concerned, is limited to the immediate neighborhood, for if shipped elsewhere the coal would pass through competitive coal basins (Kladno, Plzeň, Most); thus the Falknov coal is at a disadvantage apart from the fact that its quality is on the whole inferior when compared with other grades of lignite which compete with it at home. In consequence of these circumstances Germany has become the chief market for the Falknov coal, the nearest country, Bavaria, being the largest purchaser.

The possibility of marketing lignite in Germany was one of the chief factors in the development of Czech lignite fields the output of which increased from 6 to almost 23 million tons between 1880 and 1913. In 1913 the exports to Germany amounted to 6.54 million tons of lignite and 140,000 tons of briquettes, or almost 30 per cent of the total output of the lignite fields of northern Bohemia, and about 60 per cent of the output of the Falknov basin.

These figures do not show the total exports of lignite. Considerable quantities were exported also to the territories of former Austria, in the first place to Upper and Lower Austria, where the industries used the Bohemian lignite. These exports amounted to about 950,000 tons annually.

The factors which influenced the markets for the Czech coal before the war will again become operative as soon as normal economic conditions have been restored. This naturally applies also to the imports of foreign coal, namely German, into the Czechoslovak Republic.

The geographical situation has made possible, on the one hand, the exportation of Czechoslovak lignite, and, on the other hand, the importation of large quantities of coal into Czechoslovakia, especially from Upper and Lower Silesia. The exact amount of coal imported into Czechoslovak territory before the war cannot be ascertained for the official statistics relate to the whole territory of the former Austrian Empire. It is estimated that about seven million tons of German coal was consumed annually in the territory now occupied by the Czechoslovak Republic.

The war conditions brought about a substantial change in the imports as well as in the exports of coal. Germany needed more coal because the imports from England had ceased and the German industries and German shipping had to depend on German coal, some of which also had to be exported to neutral countries. In consequence, the exports of German coal to Austria were restricted, and thus also the exports of lignite from the Czech fields to Germany had to be reduced. The disastrous shortage of coal after the war, due to the decrease of the output on account of the diminished working capacity of the miners, did not permit an immediate return to normal conditions in the coal industry as they had existed before the war. The imports and exports of coal were far below the peace figures and the fluctuation of the currencies also hampered the coal trade. In 1921 the total exports of lignite from Czechoslovakia to Germany and Austria were only 4.67 million tons, the exports of coal were

1.23 million tons, and the exports of coke, 300,798 tons. The imports in the same year were only 847,000 tons of coal and 115,000 tons of coke. The low exports and the industrial crisis of 1922 brought about a slight decrease in employment at the mines, and, consequently, a slight decrease in the output of coal and coke.

In 1923, however, the coal industry was benefited greatly by the general improvement in the Czechoslovak trade. There are reasons to hope that the situation will improve still more, owing to the 20 per cent reduction in the price of coal which was brought about in October, 1923, as a result of reductions in wages and a lowering of the coal tax.

VI

WATER POWER

EMIL ZIMMLER, COUNCILLOR OF THE MINISTRY OF PUBLIC WORKS

The Czechoslovak Republic has an abundance of water power which is a potential source of great wealth for the country. The Republic is situated on the high European watershed between the North and the Baltic Seas on the one side, and the Mediterranean and the Black Seas on the other, with mountains standing across the direction of the currents of damp air coming from the ocean, so that the country is well watered. The Labe (Elbe), the Odra (Oder), the Morava (March), as well as many rivers rising in Slovakia and Ruthenia, tributaries of the Danube or the Tisa, all originate in Czechoslovakia and flow to the seas mentioned above. The waters of Bohemia come from the mountain valleys, gather into rivers, and leave the country at one place, thus forming a network of water-courses which requires a systematic regulation of the whole problem of water power and especially of its exploitation.

The average annual rainfall in Czechoslovakia is 740 millimetres.

	Maximum	Average	Minimum
Bohemia	850	682	505
Moravia	930	667	591
Silesia	1,145	873	763
Slovakia and Ruthenia	...	810	...

The annual flow of water is as follows: The Labe (Elbe) at Dečín: maximum 15 billion cubic metres, average 10 billion, minimum 5 billion; the Morava at Břeclava: maximum 6.8 billion, average 3.5 billion, minimum 1.57 billion; the Odra at Bohumin: maximum 2.5 billion, average 1.5 billion, minimum 1.0 billion; the Danube at Dévín: maximum 88 billion, average 59 billion, minimum 46 billion cubic meters.

In the running of grist-mills, and washing machines and stamping mills in mines, water power has been used as a source of energy ever since the twelfth century. Water power was exploited by the great lords of Bohemia who built large ponds for that purpose, especially in southern and eastern Bohemia. They also built canals connecting the rivers such as the Opatovice canal, from Hradec to Kladruby, and the Lány canal from the Cidlina river to the Labe, which are still used. These canals are monumental works of the engineers of those times.

About 13,000 establishments in Czechoslovakia use water power, estimated at 160,000 HP. Of these 7,443 are situated in Bohemia, 1,945 in Moravia, 615 in Silesia, 2,542 in Slovakia and 543 in Ruthenia. Water power has largely promoted the development of the textile industry in northern and northeastern Bohemia from Liberec to Káchov, and of other industries in western and northern Moravia and Silesia.

The progress of the natural and the technical sciences as well as the development of the hydroelectric plants have led to a new progress in the installation of water powers. Toward the end of the nineteenth century the work connected with the canalization of the Vltava and the Labe between Prague and Ustí, and of the middle Labe between Jaromer and Mélník, was begun and the construction of canals was planned to connect the Vltava (at Budejovice) with the Danube (near Vienna or Linz), and the Labe (at Pardubice, through Prerov) with the Danube (near Vienna; now near Devín) and with the Odra (near Kozlí) and the Vistula (near Cracow). The regulation of smaller rivers in Bohemia was also planned.

The regulation of the waterways was intended not only to make the rivers navigable but also to drain and irrigate the whole area. About twenty years ago, Frant. Krızík, the inventor of the arclight, worked out a plan for the development of the water powers of the middle Labe between Jaroméř and Mélník, which would yield 20,000 HP per 24 h. The system was to consist of about 20 hydroelectric plants with only two auxiliary steam plants and was to supply power to the valley of the middle Labe which is both highly fertile and highly industrialized. This project is now being carried out in a form modified, of course, by the progress of time and changed conditions. The main source of water power in Bohemia is the Vltava River from the Sumava down to Melník, especially in the mountainous valley from Vyssi Brod to Stechovice above Prague. The river has a slope of 1:1,000 with numerous rapids. It rushes through a narrow gorge in archæan rocks almost bare of dwellings where it is possible to raise the water level about 50 meters, and thus gain at least 80,000 HP per 24 h. as well as make the river navigable.

At the present time the project of developing the

water power of the Vltava between Stéchovice and Kamyk, with the St. John's rapids, is under consideration. It is estimated that the development will yield about 350 million KWH annually. The Vltava is being made navigable for ships of 700 tons from Stéchovice to Prague, and is already navigable for 1,000 ton steamers from Prague to Mélník. The Labe River from Mélník to Ústí also affords opportunity for building hydroelectric power stations at 15 locks to supply power to factories in Prague, Ústí, and the neighborhood. At present, an electric power station is being constructed at Střekov near Ústí which will supply 90 million KWH annually to various industries, especially the chemical industry. On the middle Labe several plants are in operation and five hydroelectric power stations are in process of construction.

The two largest rivers of Bohemia, the Labe and the Vltava, the former flowing through a plain, the latter through mountains, form the backbone for a systematic development of the water powers of the country. The fact that the high-pressure sites of the middle Vltava can be coupled up with the low-pressure sites of the Labe is especially favorable. These main lines will be connected with the water powers of the tributaries which have high pressure in the mountainous regions of their origin, and low pressure in the plains, like the rivers Jizera, Chrudimka, Sázava, Berounka, Otava, Luznice and Malse. The Vltava in the south, and the Jizera in the north, with an annual rainfall as high as 1,000 mm, and with frequent water falls, offer a number of suitable sites for the development of water power.

Due to the admirably regular distribution of the river net in Bohemia and Moravia the water powers are uniformly distributed throughout the country. These powers can be of service to all the inhabitants, for the power plants will encircle the whole country along the border mountains and the sources of the tributary rivers. This circle is diametrically connected by a cross, formed by the cross-country flow of the Vltava and the lower Labe from the south to the north, and by the middle Labe and the Berounka from east to west.

The water powers will be considerably enhanced and enlarged by storage reservoirs, which can be safely constructed in the valleys composed largely of archæan rocks. The geological survey of Bohemia has shown that in the mountainous districts reservoirs with a total capacity of 1,600 million cubic meters can be built, large enough to equalize the flow of the rivers and thus prevent disastrous floods. In Bohemia, on the Berounka river near the castle of Křivoklát, between Prague and Plzeň, about 600 million cubic meters of water can be impounded by the construction of a masonry dam 60 meters high; the reservoir would improve the flow of the Vltava and the Labe for a distance reaching far into Germany. Navigation would also gain and the effectiveness of all water-power plants would be increased. This reservoir would be the largest of its kind in Europe. The coal mines situated in the neighborhood of the water-power stations will supply low-cost fuel for the auxiliary steam plants, the combination permitting an ideal solution of the problem of a regular supply of power.

Thus nature itself comes to the aid of the engineer, enabling him at a low cost to construct an efficient system for the development of water power and the distribution of energy. There is no doubt that sufficient power will be provided for the manufacturing industries, for agriculture, and the people in general, at a very low cost—a great advantage in international competition.

The country has been exhausted by the war, but the work of power development and electrification is proceeding rapidly, for it is generally recognized that, under the conditions described above, a power plant is a highly productive and profitable investment. In some districts of Bohemia, particularly along the middle Labe, electricity has already largely supplanted expensive human labor not only in the factories but also on the farms.

In Moravia the conditions are similarly favorable. Almost the whole province belongs to the basin of the Morava river which carries all the drainage of the country, with the sole exception of the Odra, southward to the Danube. The Morava, flowing through a wide plateau from north to south, offers a series of low-pressure water powers, some of which are under construction (Kromeriz, 3,000 HP; Hodonin, 1,000 HP, etc.). Additional power can be developed on its tributaries, the Bečva, the Bystřička, and others.

The course of the Dyje (Thaya) resembles that of the Bohemian Vltava. Flowing from west to east in a gorge of metamorphic rocks, the Dyje offers high-pressure sites. By a masonry dam below Vranov 180 million cubic meters of water will be impounded, and the entire course of the Dyje to its junction with the Morava will be controlled; the truck farms in the valley will be protected against floods and at the same time provided with a regular supply of water for irrigation purposes; in four reaches of the river 16,316 HP will be developed, producing 100 million kwh per annum. The tributaries of the Dyje also offer sites suitable for the construction of reservoirs and the development of about 13,700 HP.

By impounding about 700 million cubic meters of water in storage reservoirs in Moravia it will become possible to regulate the discharge of the Morava basin, enlarge the water powers and connect them by a high-tension line along the frontiers as well as diagonally. The coal mines of Rosice and Oslavany in western Moravia and the great coal fields of Ostrava in the northeast will supply the auxiliary steam plants. These conditions assure an economical development and profitable exploitation of the water powers available in Moravia.

Silesia, divided in two unequal parts by the northeast extension of Moravia, offers workable water-power sites in the Sudetes mountains in the west. The conditions are less favorable in the eastern part of the country. The Sudetes consist of gneisses and other crystalline rocks, while limestone and sandstone formations predominate in the Carpathians of eastern Silesia where the great porosity of the soil, the greater rapidity of disintegration, and the movement of boulders and gravel are serious hindrances to water-power development. These conditions are very similar to those prevailing in the Austrian Alps where the construction of reservoirs is almost impossible. Nevertheless, more than 30 sites suitable for reservoirs have been surveyed in Silesia, and 12 reservoirs are planned to feed the Odra and improve its flow far into Germany. Work has been commenced on the dams at Zimrovice and Kružberk, near Opava and Krnov, which will provide about 40,000 HP for the textile and the metallurgical industries and supply water to the mines and iron mills of Vitkovice, Ostrava and Bohumin in the Karvin-Ostrava coal basin, the most highly industrialized region of Moravia and Silesia.

In the aggregate, about 120,000 HP is available in Moravia and Silesia, with about 33,000 HP developed. Plans have been prepared for the immediate development of 84,000 HP.

Slovakia, long neglected by the former regime, has been carefully surveyed for water-power sites. The steep slopes of its rivers and the large volume of water carried by them give Slovakia the first place among the provinces of the Czechoslovak Republic in water-power resources. The potential water power is estimated as 775,000 HP, with only 35,000 HP developed. The limestone formation of the Carpathians and the resulting movement of gravel offer certain obstacles, but the extensive valleys permit the construction of lateral canals, flumes, and conduits to concentrate the falls, and the installation of hydroelectric plants in an unbroken series along some of the rivers, particularly the Vah (Waag). The flow will be improved by a storage reservoir for 280 million cubic meters of water at Trstenice, near the frontier of Poland. The valleys, extending from the Carpathians to the Danube in parallel lines, and dotted with iron mills, paper mills, and industrial cities, will be connected by primary lines over the mountain ridges and provided with a network of distributing lines. The auxiliary plants will use petroleum from the Gbely oil fields, or coal from Ostrava or local mines. Two great potential sources of water power are the Danube which forms the boundary between Slovakia and Austria and Hungary, and the lower Morava, from Břeclava to Dévín, forming the boundary between Slovakia and Austria.

By the peace treaties of St. Germain, article 306, and of Trianon, article 290, the Czechoslovak Republic was given an exclusive right to develop water power on the border rivers on authorization by the International Danube Commission. Czechoslovakia will doubtless utilize this right to its fullest extent, especially on that part of the Danube near Bratislava, where, under the Trianon Treaty, it controls both banks. It will not be difficult to utilize the water power of the main stream of the river, and also that of the long arm of Nové Zámky which diverges from the main stream below Bratislava and after a course of 103 kilometers again joins the Danube near Komárno. The fall of this arm is 29 meters; it can easily produce 250,000 H P, which would yield 750 million KWH annually for the city of Bratislava and the vicinity with its ports, railroads, industries, and farms.

Ruthenia, which has very fertile lowlands in the southern part and mountains and forests in the northern part, offers suitable sites in the northern districts.

The rivers flow almost parallel from the Carpathians to the Tisa river and are at present used for the floating of timber. Some important weirs have been constructed here to regulate the flow of water. The potential water power in Ruthenia is estimated at about 227,000 HP, of which at present only about 4,000 HP is utilized. The project, which is now under consideration, contemplates the construction of one of the largest plants in Czechoslovakia, that is, the connection of the rivers Rika and Terblje by a conduit for the erection of a hydrocentral with a capacity of 44,000 HP. Power plants with a total capacity of 50,000 HP are planned which will fully supply the local demand.

On the basis of surveys as explained in the foregoing, the water power resources of the Czechoslovak Republic may conservatively be estimated as follows:

	Potential Horse power	Developed Horse power
Bohemia	500,000	90,000
Moravia and Silesia	120,000	33,000
Slovakia	775,000	30,000
Ruthenia	227,000	4,000
Total	1,622,000	157,000

It will be seen that only ten per cent of the available water power is utilized at present. This water power would yield at the distribution switchboard 5.5 million Kwh annually. This power will be substantially increased when the extensive program of development which is being prepared has been carried out and when the geological survey of Slovakia and Ruthenia has been completed. In the meantime, hydrocentrals are being constructed by the Government and by municipal corporations, on the principle that if low-cost energy is to be placed at the service of the people, it must be under the control of the public.

The State is now building 10 hydro-electric power stations at a cost of about 136 million Czechoslovak crowns, the provinces (Bohemia, Moravia) are constructing 6 power stations at a cost of about 75 million Czechoslovak crowns; in the budget for 1922 the State provided 50 million and the provinces 42 million Czechoslovak crowns for the hydrocentrals. It should be mentioned that the Republic is financing the development with its own funds.

For the water powers which can be developed in the immediate future as soon as the necessary appropriations become available, the State, the provinces and the municipal corporations have prepared the following projects:

	Horse power
Bohemia	285,369
Moravia	33,923
Silesia	39,213
Slovakia	20,889
Carpathian Ruthenia	46,340
Total	425,734

at a cost of about 2.6 billion Czechoslovak crowns.

The financial success of hydro-electric plants naturally depends on an adequate and constant consumption, and an economical organization of the distribution and sale of the current.

There can be no doubt that the consumption of current will increase. Czechoslovakia possesses about

75 per cent of the industries of former Austria and is an exporting country; the people are well informed, hard-working and progressive. The demand for low-cost energy increases as human labor becomes too expensive. Many of our farmers who have used electricity for years have declared that they can not do without it; and low-cost energy is indispensable to manufacturing industries in the present conditions of international competition.

In 1913 engineer Vladimir List estimated the consumption of current in Bohemia for that year at 1,800 million KWH, and for Moravia at 370 million. If we add about 830 million for Silesia, Slovakia and Ruthenia, the consumption of current for the year 1913 would have been about 3 billion KWH, which could have been fully supplied by water power. According to present indications, consumption will increase as soon as the conditions, especially in eastern Europe, have again become normal, and trade has returned to its former channels.

The supply of energy and the distribution of power are in the hands of special organizations. The country is divided into fifteen districts; Bohemia into six, Moravia and Silesia into four, Slovakia and Ruthenia into five. In each district mixed corporations, associations, or cooperative societies have been organized, in which the State, the provinces, counties, communes, and large industrial establishments are shareholders. These organizations provide the current, that is, they rent the power stations, particularly the hydrocentrals, or obtain power from the plants owned by the State or the provinces, and distribute and sell power to large consumers or to organizations which sell the current to minor consumers.

The associations organized thus far have achieved very good results. The following table shows their operating capital:

	Total	State and municipal
	(in million Czecho-slovak crowns)	
Bohemia	119	105
Moravia and Silesia	59	25
Slovakia and Ruthenia	28	12
	206	142

This movement was initiated by the Government. Less than nine months after the establishment of the Czechoslovak Republic, on July 22, 1919, a law was passed in support of electrification, and the foundation was laid for the carrying out of the first part of the program. The Government granted a subsidy of 120,000,000 Czechoslovak crowns to enterprises of public utility which were assisted also by the removal of various legal and financial obstacles, the Government, however, retaining the right of supervision. The Czechoslovak Government is fully aware of the great importance of water power and is working energetically for a proper solution of the problems of development and an effective utilization of that valuable resource.

VII

INDUSTRY

Dr. Karel Franzl, Editor of "The Czechoslovak Compass," Prague

The development of industry is everywhere closely associated with political, historical and social conditions, as well as with the natural conditions of the country.

In Czechoslovakia the historical and political conditions favored the progress of the German industry. German immigrants had been coming to Czechoslovakia since time immemorial, at first mainly from the vicinity of the lower Rhine. These German immigrants, together with the German nobility and the industrial policies of the government in the seventeenth and particularly in the eighteenth and nineteenth centuries, were mainly responsible for the advanced position of the German industry in Czechoslovakia as compared with the Czech and the Slovak industry.

The Czech nation, deprived not only of its political independence, but likewise of the most intelligent and the most enterprising and active industrial classes by the terrible consequences of the battle of the White Mountain (1620), and by the subsequent religious persecution, Germanization, and feudal oppression carried on for centuries, entered the nineteenth century only a remnant of a nation, but happily composed of sturdy peasants. The emancipation of the peasants begun by Emperor Joseph's reforms and fully accomplished in the period 1848 to 1879, with the freedom of occupations, obtained in 1858, gave the Czech peasants freedom of movement and freedom in the choice of occupation, offered them the possibility to enter government service, to engage in industries and commerce, and thus to free themselves from German influence and predominance and to build up the Czech national community. In Slovakia the work of undoing the consequences of a thousand years of oppression of the Slovak branch of the Czechoslovak nation is still in the beginning. Notwithstanding these historical conditions, the Czechs have succeeded in numerous branches of industry and commerce and the Slovaks, too, are making favorable progress.

Among the natural conditions of industrial production, the natural resources and water as a source of power are of foremost importance. Czechoslovakia is richly wooded, has plenty of coal and other minerals and raw materials, and has an excellent agriculture which nearly covers the needs of the home population, so that only wheat needs to be imported. The importance of the Czechoslovak countries in this respect is indicated in the following table, showing the imports and exports of Czechoslovakia in 1920 in comparison with the foreign trade of Austria-Hungary in 1914:

	Czechoslovakia in 1920 Imports	Exports	Austria-Hungary in 1914 Imports	Exports
1. Raw materials—				
quintals.........	30,808,745	55,529,729	159,637,941	104,722,173
pieces...........	24,550	1,336	123,061	128,061
2. Semi-manufactures—				
quintals.........	2,850,406	5,493,180	4,724,614	22,455,538
3. Manufactures—				
quintals.........	5,442,407	7,999,230	5,432,959	14,773,734
pieces...........	231,252	2,645,532	2,347,234	6,961,417
tons (ships).....	10	...	381	9,657
Total—				
quintals.........	39,101,558	69,022,139	169,805,514	141,951,445
pieces...........	255,802	2,646,868	2,470,295	7,089,478
tons (ships).....	10	...	381	9,657

In 1914 Austria-Hungary imported 159.6 millions of quintals of raw materials, *i.e.,* 94 per cent of the total imports, and exported 104.7 million quintals of raw materials, *i.e.,* 74 per cent of the total exports. The imports were 55 million quintals more than the exports. In 1920 Czechoslovakia imported 30.8 million quintals of raw materials, *i.e.,* 78.8 per cent of the total imports, and exported 55.5 million quintals, *i.e.,* 80.5 per cent of the total exports, exporting therefore, 24.75 million quintals or 80.4 per cent of raw materials more than it had imported. The chief articles of exports were supplied by the natural wealth, for two-thirds of the exports was coal and wood. The exports of coal and wood in 1920 were 51.8 million quintals, and the imports 13.2 million quintals only. There is an abundance of lignite, the exports of which in 1920 were 33.89 million quintals, and the imports 0.4 million quintals only.

Minerals other than coal were second in the exports in 1920, totaling 5.02 million quintals, and including 1.8 million quintals of china clay and 0.84 million quintals of other clays, 0.43 million quintals of iron ore, 0.45 million quintals of limestone, 0.17 million quintals of lime, 0.22 million quintals of sand, 0.2 million quintals of magnesite, 0.12 million quintals of graphite, etc. The total imports of ores were 9.27 million quintals, an excess of 4.25 million quintals over exports. The imports of iron ore alone were 5.63 million quintals (3.33 from Sweden, 1.22 from Germany, 1.05 from Austria).

The chief iron mines are situated in the districts of Nucice, Jinočany, Krabulov Zdice (Prazská Zelezářská Spolecnost), Ejpovice, in the Gemer district (Akciové Železarny in Hrádek), in Nižní Medzev (Abauj-Turna district in Slovakia), in the Spiš district in the vicinity of Gelnice and Slovinek (Rimamuraňsko-salgotarjanska Zelezarská), in Krompachy (Pohernadská železoprůmyslová) and in Prakovce, Government-owned iron mines are situated in Zelezník, Rudné and Nadabule near Rožnava in the Gemer district in Slovakia. Crude sulphur is mined in Cajle, copper ore in Casté near Pezinok (Bratislava district), in Dobsine (Gemer district) and in Vernerovice (Broumov district). Government-owned silver and lead mines are in Příbram; gold, silver, lead and copper mines in Baňská Stiavnice; gold and silver mines in Hodrus, Finsterort and Vyhen (Tekov district), gold and silver and antimony mines in Magurka (Tékov district) and Zlata Ida (Abauj-Turna district). There is also a gold mine in Cajle near Pezinok (Bratislava district); antimony is extracted in Millsorsko; lead is found in Chvalovice near Netolice in Bohemia, in Bradno and Rovné in the Gemer district in Slovakia; magnesite in the Gemer area in Chyžná Voda, in Jelsava, Ochtiné and Hnušté near Košice and in Lovinobáni (Novohrad district);

the annual output is about 102,000 metric tons, of which about 20,000 tons is used at home and the remainder exported. The government-owned salt mines at Solnohrad near Prešov in Slovakia and at Akna Slatina in the Marmaroš district in Ruthenia should also be mentioned, as well as the opal mines in Dubnik near Prešov, and the naphtha wells at Gbely in the Nitra district of Slovakia.

The Bohemian iron industry is of very ancient origin. Iron foundries and forges, although small, were numerous in Bohemia in the fourteenth and fifteenth centuries. They were located in forests and in places where iron ore was found and many of them are still in operation, as for example the Stará Huť pod Hýskovem near the city of Beroun, the forges in Králův Dvůr near Beroun, etc. At present the most important iron foundries are in Kladno (Pražská Železářská) in Hradek Komarov near Rokycany, in Rotava-Nejdek, in Třinec and in Vıtkovice. In Slovakia there are government-owned foundries in Tisovéc, Krompachy, Prakovce near Gelnice and in Ztratené. Out of the 47 blast furnaces located in the former Austrian Empire 27 with an annual capacity of 1.5 million tons are now situated in the Czechoslovak Republic. Owing to the industrial crisis their output was reduced to about one-fifth of their normal capacity.

Steel foundries are located in Vítkovice, Kladno, Hrádek u Rokycan, Chomutov, Krompachy, Trnava and Nadest, other foundries in Hronec (government-owned), Holonkov, Dobřiva, Sobotin, Stépánov, etc. In 1919, 786.022 tons of steel were produced. In 1918 the steel foundries of Czechoslovakia produced 58 per cent of the total output of Austria-Hungary.

The engineering industry, to the development of which intensive agriculture and the agricultural industries have contributed greatly, is concentrated chiefly in the large cities and their neighborhood. The electrotechnical industry and the manufacture of fine mechanical goods are also concentrated in the larger cities. The chief centers of these industries are Prague, Plzeň, Hradec Kralove, Brno, Prostéjov, Moravská Ostrava, Bratislava, Košice, Lučenec, Prešov, Sered nad Váhom, Rimavská Sobota and numerous less important places. Together with the factories manufacturing automobiles, motor plows, locomotives, railway cars and special machines, this industry employs 150,000 workmen, and when fully employed, produces over 1,000,000 tons of goods in a year. It occupies a foremost position in the manufacture of machinery and equipment for sugar mills, distilleries and breweries, and also manufactures and exports benzine and naphtha motors, motor plows, steam boilers and engines, and cranes. The production of musical and surgical instruments is also noteworthy. The unfavorable side of the Czechoslovak engineering industry is its insufficient specialization. Although possessing a large engineering industry, Czechoslovakia still must import various textile printing machines, machines needed in the dairy industry, or in the manufacture of matches, certain metal-working machines, etc. The factories manufacturing agricultural machinery number about 150 and are located in the central districts of Bohemia, and in the neighborhood of Prostéjov, Ṕrerov and Trnava in

Moravia. Some of these establishments export as much as 90 per cent of their output, now chiefly to the Balkans and France.

Considerable quantities of goods are exported by the enamel-ware factories located in Prague, Hořovice, Komárov, Stará Huť u Dobříše, Plzeň, Petržalka u Bratislavy, Matějovice in the Spiš county and in Filakov and Lučenec in the county of Nové Hrady in Slovakia. They export from 80 to 90 per cent of their output.

Buttons and small metal articles, needles, and footwear accessories are also manufactured extensively. These industries are concentrated mainly in the vicinity of greater Prague, Podmoklí, Jablonec nad Jizerou (Gablonz) and in the Czech part of Silesia.

The development of the Czech electrotechnical industry, originating in 1860, was promoted by the inventions of Czech electrotechnicians. The manufacture of machinery for the generation and utilization of power is centered chiefly in Prague and its vicinity, in Podmoklí, Brno, Mohelnice and Bratislava; the manufacture of other apparatus and appliances in Prague, Jablonné nad Orlicí and Olomouc. The manufacture of cables, insulated wires and pipes is concentrated in Prague, Podmoklí and Bratislava; the manufacture of small electric appliances in Prague, Radotín, Mladá Boleslav; electric lighting fixtures are made in Prague, Liberec, and the neighboring districts.

The electric lamp industry which, until recently, was carried on by small enterprises is now represented by three large concerns (located in Hloubětín, Přívoz and

Prague). There are about 360 power plants in Czechoslovakia.

The various branches of industry participated in 1920 in Czechoslovak imports and exports as follows:

	Imports	Exports
Iron and steel, and manufactures of (quintals)	1,147,900	1,639,265
Nonferrous metals and manufactures of (quintals)	287,022	46,010
Machinery (quintals)	299,178	403,824
Electrical machinery and apparatus (quintals)	56,505	11,209
Vehicles (quintals)	239,775	13,502
(pieces)	1,190	6,626
tons (ships)	10	......
Instruments and watches (quintals)	6,500	13,691
(pieces)	32,422	41

It has already been stated that the development of the important branches of industries, especially the engineering and the chemical industries, was greatly advanced by the expansion of the sugar, brewing, and distillery industries. The development of the brewing industry was very rapid in the sixties of the last century. At that time also many sugar refineries were founded, some even in places where the conditions were unfavorable, so that many of them had to be abandoned after their first campaign. Work in other refineries had to be stopped after the general crisis of 1873 and in the sugar crisis of 1884. In spite of this, however, the sugar industry has remained one of the main exporting industries, and the Czech sugar is, perhaps with the exception of Bohemian glass, the best-known Czechoslovak product in the world market. In 1919, there were in Czechoslovakia 164 sugar factories and 11 refineries. Of these concerns 113 are situated in Bohemia, 48 in Moravia, 6 in Silesia and 8 in Slovakia. The largest sugar factory is in Trnava, Slovakia, producing about 20,000 quintals of beet sugar per 24 hours or 2 million quintals annually. In the other factories the output varies from 5,000 to 10,000 quintals.

The Czechoslovak alcohol industry, one of the exporting industries, shows a remarkable development, especially since 1860. In Czechoslovakia there are 989 agricultural distilleries producing 167,860 hectoliters; Moravia 163, producing 90,250 hectoliters; Silesia 100, producing 42,100 hectoliters. Of the industrial distilleries there are 19 in Bohemia, 8 in Moravia, 6 in Silesia, 33 in Slovakia. Of the 48 refineries of alcohol, 29 are engaged in the production of alcohol. The largest annual output of the agricultural distilleries in the years from 1910 to 1920 amounted to 741,180 hectoliters. The industrial distilleries produced 306,818 hectoliters of alcohol in 1920-21.

The manufacture of liqueurs, vinegar, and fruit juices and essences has made a noteworthy progress. Liqueurs are produced both by large and small concerns. There are 30 large establishments engaged in this industry. Fruit wines are produced by 24 concerns, the yearly output of which amount to 10,000 hectoliters. The greater part of the fruit wines is exported to northern Europe. In 77 establishments, of which 11 are large ones, 3,800 tons of fruit juices are produced annually; one-fourth of the output is consumed at home. The foreign demand for these products is best illustrated by the following figures: in 1920, 125,774 quintals of alcohol were exported; 30,994 quintals of liqueurs, punch essences, and other alcoholic beverages containing sugar or other substances; 5,111 quintals of other distilled beverages; 1,754 quintals of cognac; 2,694 quintals of arrack and rum; 713 quintals of brandy; 982 quintals of vinegar; 10,985 quintals of fruit wines, wine and fruit cider, fruit juices and essences, and beverages made from honey.

In Bohemia the production of beer is of ancient origin. Beer was first prepared privately at home, then, from the fourteenth to the end of the eighteenth century, it was produced in commercial quantities on a small scale. With the technical and industrial progress in the nineteenth century, the production of beer developed into an important industry. In 1841, there were in Bohemia 1,052 breweries, but in 1915-1916 only 475 of them remained, for the competition of large breweries situated near the big cities had forced the breweries located in the country out of business. The Bohemian breweries are known for their modern equipment and the quality of their beer. There are 663 breweries in Czechoslovakia, of which 54 belong to stock companies, 18 to other corporations and the remainder are privately owned. At present the breweries employ about 20,000 workmen. Before the war there were 23 large breweries producing over 100,000 hectoliters each, the medium-sized breweries produced from 15,000 to 100,000 hectoliters, and the small breweries up to 15,000 hectoliters of beer. In 1911, the brewery of Plzeň (Méštanský pivovar), famous for its world-known beer, produced 969,121 hectoliters, and the brewery of Smíchov over 600,000 hectoliters. In 1920, the exports of beer amounted to 295,002 quintals and were directed chiefly to Germany and Austria; the imports of beer were 57,743 quintals.

There are 203 malt factories in Czechoslovakia, of which 35 are controlled by stock companies and 168 are privately owned. Barley from the Haná district (Moravia) and Slovak barley are known for their excellent qualities; the barley grown in central Bohemia is also of excellent quality. The Czechoslovak malt successfully competes with the German malt. The exports of malt in 1920 amounted to 630,421 quintals, and went chiefly to Italy, Austria, Germany, Switzerland, Belgium, Norway, France and South America.

The production of potato starch, dextrin, syrup and glucose is concentrated mostly in the hilly borderland along the frontier of Bohemia and Moravia and in the Nitra, Tékov and Spiš districts of Slovakia.

The dairy industry is chiefly in the hands of co-operative farmers' associations. The largest dairies are located near Prague. Cheese is made mostly in Moravia and Slovakia (Brynza, Liptava and other brands of cheese are made chiefly in the districts of Liptava, Zvolen and Trenčin).

Noteworthy is the manufacture of candies and chocolate, which has an abundant supply of sugar and fruit. There are 80 establishments of which 25 make chocolate and cacao powder. The present annual output, which is still below the normal production, is about 40,000 tons, of which about 60 per cent is exported.

The manufacture of marmalade grew rapidly during the war. There are 420 establishments (40 large ones) with an annual capacity of 36,000 tons. Fruit comfits are made in 5 factories. There are 70 establishments for drying chicory, located mostly in Bohemia, which was the chief producer of chicory in former Austria. The chicory is prepared in 40 establishments (15 larger ones) consuming 60,000 tons of chicory and producing 30,000 tons of dried chicory root. Coffee substitutes prepared from rye and barley are produced in 30 establishments, the output of which is about 20,000 tons annually. Large establishments for making sauerkraut number 19, and their yearly output is 8,000 tons. During the war, the preparation of vegetables and canned meat attained considerable extent. The dill pickles of Znojmo and Zatec are known for their excellent quality. In Prague and in southern Bohemia the smoked meat industry is located, the Prague hams being known the world over. There are 11 establishments for the preparation of fish imported from the North and the Baltic Seas.

In the flour milling industry a gradual process of transformation of small establishments into large ones is now under way. There are about 10,750 mills capable of grinding 173,000 quintals of grain in twenty-four hours, or about 52,500,000 quintals yearly. 5,280 of these mills, with a capacity of 80,610 quintals, are in Bohemia, 2,100 are in Moravia (45,000 quintals), 337 in Silesia (7,300 quintals) and 3,000 in Slovakia (40,00 quintals). In Ruthenia, with but a few mills, this industry is still undeveloped. The largest mills are found in Velký Šaryš, Greater Prague,

Lucenec, Nitra, Bratislava, Rosice, Bohumin and Brnénec near Polička. Bread is made mostly in small bakeries, but large baking concerns and workingmen's coöperative organizations are gradually taking the place of the small bakeries. As regards the preparation of pastry, the Lomnice biscuits and the Hořice rolls deserve to be mentioned. The exports of pastry were 3,763 quintals in 1920. Noteworthy is also the preparation of macaroni and noodles, which are exported chiefly to England. The exports of these products in 1920 were 1,018 quintals.

One of the oldest branches of Czechoslovak industry is the manufacture of glass. The first glass works in Bohemia were founded in the early eleventh century by a nobleman, Gunther. In the fourteenth and fifteenth centuries, glass bearing a slight green tinge was produced in the wooded districts of the Šumava, the Ore mountains, and the Krkonoše. In the sixteenth century, glass was already cut and ground. At that time the manufacture of glass was penetrating from the borders into the interior of the land. In the fifteenth century a glass factory was established in Prague. In the sixteenth century there were glass works at Falknov, Nejdek, Turnov, Cheb, Domažlice and in other places, especially near the Moravian frontier. In 1598, Emperor Rudolf II built a glass factory in Prague near the Emperor's mill. Since the end of the sixteenth century Bohemian hollow glass and pressed glass have been known for their purity, briliancy and transparency, the qualities which made Bohemian glass famous. Today Czechoslovakia has 130 glass factories, producing hollow, cast and cut glass, plate glass, photographic glass, glass tubes, watch crystals, glass for lighting fixtures, and bottles. Besides this there are seventeen factories producing colored and special glass. In 3,000 finishing establishments the raw glass is cut, engraved, etched, painted, etc. Glass refineries are concentrated mostly in Bor (Hajdy) and Senov, and the manufacture of glass jewelry in Jablonec n-N. (Gablonz). On the whole, however, the glass works remain mostly in their ancient location. In Slovakia, glass works are located in the vicinity of Nové Hrady, Tékov and Gemer. The glass-grinding establishments are located in Bratislava. In Moravia the principal glass factories are at Kyjov, Rosice, Lužice, Velký Losín, and glass-grinding factories in Brno.

The exports of glass and glassware in 1920 were 1,400,771 quintals. The exports of porcelain in 1920 were 155,112 quintals, valued at 197 million crowns; in 1921 the exports were 213,333 quintals, valued at 313 million Czechoslovak crowns. The porcelain industry is concentrated mostly in the neighborhood of Karlovy Vary, but there are also other ceramic factories, numbering about 200. This branch of industry exports about 70 per cent of its products in normal times. The manufacture of artistic pottery, carried on in peasant homes in eastern Moravia and elsewhere, should also be mentioned. The growth of the cities provides a steady market for building materials and ceramic products used for buildings. In 1920 there were about 3,000 establishments of this kind in the country, including brick yards, lime kilns, and cement factories.

The extensive timber resources have made possible a highly developed wood and paper industry. There are over 3,200 sawmills, of which 650 are driven by steam, 50 by electricity, and the remainder by water power. Many sawmills in Prague, in the Šumava and in Slovakia specialize in the production of shingles and wooden cases, while the sawmills in southern and eastern Bohemia, Moravia and Slovakia produce excelsior besides. The abundance of wood has given rise to an extensive manufacture of toys, boxes, furniture, go-carts, shades, parquetry and wooden cases. The most important branch of the wood industry is the manufacture of furniture, which is largely concentrated in Prague and in Moravia (Brno and Třebič). There are 50 large furniture factories and about 4,000 of smaller size. The manufacture of bent-wood furniture, working largely for foreign markets, is concentrated in Moravia (Vsetín, Hobšov, Koryčany, Frenstat and Uhersky Brod) and in Slovakia (Turčianský Sv. Martin and other places). Barrels made in Prague, Plzen, Most Duchcov, Hluboka and in Ruthenia are largely exported. The manufacture of whips is carried on chiefly in Slovakia (Uhrovce and Dolní Vestenice) and in Prague (Braník) and Předměřice n.L. In the Šumava near Kasperske Hory and Volany and in northeastern Bohemia (Nova Paka and Horicko) there is an extensive wood-turning industry manufacturing wooden faucets, wooden beads, spools and other accessories for the textile industry. Picture frames and borders are made especially in Prague and Ceske Budejovice. Shoe lasts and wooden heels are manufactured in Holice, Vlašim and Klatovy, small boxes in Orlické hory, sporting goods in Podkrkonoší and northern Moravia, cane goods in Bakov nad Jizerou and in Jindřichuv Hradec, wicker goods in Brandýs nad Labem, in Mélník, Kroměříž, Morkovicko, Vizovicko, Val. Meziří, Novoméstsko, Rožnovsko, Trenčín and Nové Mésto nad Váhom. The manufacture of cork is concentrated in Prague, Nymburk and Roudnicko.

Wood pulp is manufactured in about 80 pulp mills consuming 400,000 cubic meters of wood. These mills are chiefly in northeastern Bohemia (Vrajt, Vrchlabí, Hostinne and other places) and in Slovakia (Turč. Sv. Martin, Ruzomberk, Zilina). There are 18 establishments making chemical pulp with an annual output of 35,000 to 60,000 tons. Of these concerns 5 manufacture chemical pulp only (the most important are in Ratimov, Turc. Sv. Martin and in Zilina), while the remaining thirteen are connected with paper factories. The first paper factories in Bohemia were established in the fourteenth century by King Charles IV. In the nineteenth century the manufacture of hand-made paper from flax and cotton stock was largely reduced, while machinery production steadily increased. Paper was formerly made of wood pulp and cellulose; now it is made of wood and straw pulp to which chemical or rag pulp is added, according to the kind of paper desired. The paper factories number 76, and their annual output is estimated at 175,000 tons. In normal times the industry exports 60 per cent of the output. Seven of the paper factories manufacture paper for rotary presses (the largest are in Český Krumlov, Česká Kamonice and in Harmanec, near Banska

Bystřice), two factories make paper for illustrations, one manufactures parchment, and five concerns make cigarette paper. The manufacture of paper cigar holders in Chrást near Chrudim supplies the home market and a part of the output is exported.

All the 44 cardboard factories of former Austria-Hungary are now in Czechoslovakia, and their annual output is about 12,000 tons. With an abundance of paper the country has an extensive manufacture of paper goods, such as paper bags, cigar holders, cigarette tubes, cardboard, etc. In 1920, the exports of paper pulp, paper and paper products amounted to 766,057 quintals, the imports being only 192,836 quintals. The value of the exports had decreased from 695.4 millions Czechoslovak crowns in 1920 to 654 millions in 1921, but still exceeded the value of the imports of paper and paper goods by 528.3 million, while in 1920 there was an excess of only 469.6 million Czechoslovak crowns.

The graphic industry is highly developed and extensive. The first printing establishments in Bohemia were founded in the latter part of the fifteenth century. The progress of printing was temporarily halted by the Habsburg anti-reformation. In the years 1526-1620 there were 83 printers registered in Prague, and in 1740 only 10. With the religious liberty, freedom of the press and the technical progress of the nineteenth century a new era opened for the Bohemian graphic industry. The discoveries of Prof. Jacob Husník in modern photogravure and of the academic painter Karel Klíč in the heliogravure are worthy of mention as well as those of J. Vilím, who improved the method of reproduction (asphalt process). At the present time there are 809 printing establishments in Czechoslovakia, of which 462 are in Bohemia, 117 in Moravia, 47 in Silesia and 180 in Slovakia and Ruthenia. The printing establishments supply mostly the home needs, but the graphic institutions, especially those making cuts for reproductions receive large orders from abroad. Postal cards and pictures are also largely exported. In 1920 and 1921, the imports of literary and art works were 226.5, and 223.14 million Czechoslovak crowns, the exports 72.2 and 64.64 million Czechoslovak crowns.

The chemical industry is well developed. The largest chemical establishment, the Spolek pro chemickou a hutní výrobu v Ustí nad Labem (Corporation for Chemical and Metallurgical Production in Ustí nad Labem), was founded in 1857. The chief establishments for the manufacture of fertilizers are at Kolín, Slané, Prague, Přerov, Mor. Ostrava, Vítkovice, Sepov, Opatovice, Sered nad Váhom, Žilina, Lučenec and Kostolany. There are 25 of these establishments, and their output completely supplies the needs of the country. Many establishments are engaged in the manufacture of paints, lacquers, essences, acids, vaseline, creams, polishes, soap, candles, perfumery and other toilet articles, tar, and rubber and celluloid articles, inks, chemical paper and other chemical products, etc. The production of acetic acid is concentrated mostly in Ruthenia (Velký Bočkov) and in Dobrá Voda and Smolenice in Slovakia. There is also an important production of edible and industrial fats and oils (Lovosice, Bratislava, Pardubice,

Prague, Ustí nad Labem) and of explosives (Bratislava, Prague and Semtín). The manufacturers of fireworks and matches have organized the joint-stock company "Solo." The Czechoslovak mineral oil industry has 7 large establishments situated on the banks of the rivers Labe (Elbe), Danube, and the Odra (Pardubice, Kralupy, Kolín, Bohumín, Šumperk, Bratislava and Kežmarok). This industry imports the raw materials from abroad.

Among the products mentioned above, the group of candles, soap and wax products showed in 1921 an excess of exports amounting to 14 million crowns; matches and explosives, an excess of 77.9 million crowns.

The manufacture of leather has been carried on since the earliest times. Due to the invention of new machinery during the last thirty years, the industry has made rapid progress. Czechoslovakia has two-thirds of the total leather industry of former Austria-Hungary. There are 260 leather factories situated in Prague, Královė Hradec, Třebachovice, Trýmisté nad Orlicí, Kostelec nad Orlicí, Liberec, Česká Lípa, Chabařovice, Varnsdorf, Klatovy, Plzeň, Sušice, Písek, Tábor, Česka Skalice, Litoměřice, Budyň, Lipt. Svatý Mikuláš, Březová, Bratislava, Nové Zámky, Třebíč, Hodonín, Zlín, Olomouc.

The production of hand-made shoes in Czechoslovakia is still considerable, yet modern machinery is taking the place of hand labor. Of the daily output of the shoe industry, estimated at 80,000 pairs of shoes, about 65 per cent is made by machinery. The centers of the shoe industry are Prague, Pardubice,

Chrudím, Brno, Prostějov, Zlín and Jihlava. The glove industry is concentrated in Prague and in the Rudohoří. With the Prague glove industry is associated the home production of sewed gloves in the neighborhood of Dobříš and Příbram. Washable gloves and deerskin gloves are made in Kadaň. There are 52 glove factories and about 130 smaller establishments in the country. Before the war the exports of gloves amounted to 90 per cent of the production. Leather bags and saddles are now made mostly by machinery. Noteworthy is the manufacture of leather notions and leggings. In 1920, 28,255 quintals of leather and leather goods were exported and 24,234 quintals imported. In 1920 the value of the exports was 275.25 million crowns higher than the value of the imports, in 1921 the excess was 481.35 million crowns.

The weaving industry is well developed and consumes large quantities of cotton and flax. The center of this industry is in northern Bohemia and in the districts of Prague and Liberec. The wool industry is concentrated in Krnov and Humpolec, the flax industry in Trutnov, Rumberk and Šumperk, the silk industry in northern Moravia, the manufacture of clothing and millinery in the district of Prostějov, embroideries are made in Kraslice, Chrudím and Zábřeh, Teleč, Uh. Hradiště, Strážnice, and bobbinet laces are manufactured in the Rudohoří, and galloons and trimmings in Vejprty.

The manufacture of hats is carried on especially in Moravia (Prostějov, Boskovice, Nový Jičín), the manufacture of straw and felt hats is a home industry in the distrcits of Prostéjov, Hradištsko and Hanácko. Czechoslovakia possesses over 80 per cent of the textile industry of the former Habsburg monarchy. The Prostéjov district, with a staff of highly skilled workers, now manufactures very fine textile goods although before the war only the common grades were made there.

The following figures relating to the value of the Czechoslovak foreign trade show the importance of the textile industry (in million Czechoslovak crowns):

	1920		1921	
	Imports	Exports	Imports	Exports
Cotton, and manufactures of......	5,029.84	2,525.61	3,446.55	3,801.56
Flax, hemp, jute..................	311.35	350.96	507.40	422.41
Wool, and manufactures of........	2,211.53	6,683.76	2,125.48	4,104.01
Silk, and manufactures of.........	299.36	151.96	475.81	450.71
Clothing and millinery............	591.12	904.82	63.96	793.09

The general position of the Czechoslovak industries in 1920 is shown by the following figures of imports and exports (figures in brackets show percentages):

	Imports		Exports	
Products of agriculture, forestry, and the fisheries: quintals......	3,986,421.09	(10.2)	7,392,146.21	(10.7)
pieces.............	24,550	(9.6)	1,336	(0.1)
Mine and foundry products: quintals	26,822,324	(68.6)	48,137,583	(69.7)
Manufactures: quintals	8,292,813.52	(21.2)	13,492,410.35	(19.6)
pieces.............	231,252	(90.4)	2,645,532	(99.9)

The Czechoslovak industries still have great possibilities of development and the industrial activities of Czechoslovakia may be expected to expand when the political and economic conditions in Europe have become normal.

VIII

FOREIGN TRADE

Dr. Fr. Peroutka, Division Chief in the Ministry of Commerce

Intensive agriculture and prosperous industries have enabled Czechoslovakia to build up an extensive foreign trade. The balance of trade is, on the whole, favorable. The country has to import foodstuffs and raw materials needed in the industries, and exports industrial products in return. Many branches of industry have to seek foreign markets for as much as fifty to ninety per cent of their products.

Before the war, in the territory of the present Czechoslovak Republic, about 10.2 million metric quintals of wheat were cultivated, 15.3 million quintals of rye, and 15.2 million quintals of barley. After the war, the harvest of wheat in 1920 was 7.1 million quintals, in 1921 10,528,000 quintals, in 1922 9,150,000 quintals, but, as it is necessary to keep about 1.2 million quintals for sowing, the production does not cover home consumption (80-90 kilograms per head annually). In the case of rye (home consumption per head about 100 kilograms yearly and about 1.8 million quintals needed for sowing) Czechoslovakia would be self-supporting provided the harvest were normal. But the harvest in 1920 was only 8.2

million quintals, in 1921 13,649,000 quintals and in 1922 12,979,000 quintals.

The area sown to barley in Czechoslovakia is 40 per cent, and the crop 50 per cent, of the corresponding totals for Austria-Hungary. Barley is the principal cereal exported from Czechoslovakia. It is exported in the grain or in the form of malt; about three million quintals are exported annually. The crop of barley in 1920 was 7,980,000, in 1921 10,336,000 and in 1922 10,092,000 quintals.

With the normal production of oats, which is 16.4 million quintals, the State is self-supporting, but even in the years of poor harvests the importation of oats is not absolutely necessary, as other fodder can be substituted. The crop of oats in 1920 was 8,500,000, in 1921 10,754,000, and 1922 10,386,000 quintals.

IMPORTS OF GRAIN, FLOUR, AND RICE INTO CZECHOSLOVAKIA
(In metric quintals of 220.46 pounds)

	1920	1921	1922
Wheat	177,653	1,388,729	337,584
Rye	248,219	745,606	97,021
Barley	160	10,648	2,177
Oats	643	145,105	194,458
Corn	79,841	1,988,674	987,432
Wheat flour	1,595,608	2,775,982	2,074,643
Rye flour	39,985	77,444	146,639
Rice	240,897	6,283	411,429
Malt	3,886	3,278	46
EXPORTS			
Barley	7,441	27,365	1,349,402
Oats	113,843	36,515	2,198
Malt	630,421	283,400	553,713

The crop of sugar beets in 1920 was 47., in 1921 almost 48., and in 1922 52.4 million quintals. The production of sugar in Czechoslovakia, expressed in terms of raw, was 722,995 metric tons in the season of 1920-21; 662,928 tons in 1921-22, and 736,034 tons in 1922-23. The production of 1922-23 included 630,386 tons of refined and 17,394 tons of raw sugar. The sugar industry is well developed and has an excellent commercial and banking organization. Refined sugar is one of the principal articles of the Czechoslovak export trade.

EXPORTS OF SUGAR

	Quintals thousand	Czechoslovak (crowns) million
1920	2,400	3,405
1921	4,570	3,749
1922	3,203	1,400
1923	5,193	1,884

Other agricultural exports are hops, clover seed, grass seed, sugar beet, chicory roots, cabbages, cucumbers, fruits (early pears and apples).

	Hops harvested quintals	Exported quintals
1920	52,656	67,863
1921	28,845	30,352
1922	56,421	48,129
1923	30,900	30,963

The rich harvest of potatoes (in 1920 49 million quintals, in 1921 43,292,000 quintals, in 1922 90,692,000 quintals) is the basis for the alcohol industry and for the manufacture of starch. Alcohol is exported in large quantities to Germany and Austria. The starch industry produces about 450,000 metric tons of starch annually which is more than is needed for home consumption. The high grade of the Zatec hops and of the Czech and Moravian malting barley guarantee good qualities of beer. The total production of beer is much smaller now than before the war; the exports were 295,000 quintals in 1920; 256,800 quintals in 1921, and 71,222 quintals in 1922. Beer is exported chiefly to Germany, Italy and Austria.

Czechoslovakia imports cattle, hogs, and meat chiefly from Yugoslavia and Rumania; lard from the United States; butter from Denmark; margarine from the Netherlands; wine from Hungary, Italy, Austria, and France. In 1920, 4,198 head of cattle and 12,564 hogs were imported; in 1921 3,280 head of cattle and 26,838 hogs; and in 1922 94,762 head of cattle and 258,308 hogs. The increase in the imports in 1922 is due to a more liberal policy in matters of supply. The imports of lard and bacon were 132,354 quintals in 1920, 256,590 quintals in 1921, and 442,989 quintals in 1922. Before the war, Prague hams were largely exported. For the manufacture of artificial fats large quantities of raw material are imported (copra, palm kernels, and vegetable oils). The imports of wines amounted in 1920 to about 460,000 quintals, in 1920, about 270,000 quintals in 1921, and 165,000 quintals in 1922; the production of wine, namely in Slovakia and in Carpathian Ruthenia, is about 450,000 hectoliters annually. Czechoslovak mineral waters are exported in large quantities.

The chocolate industry imported for manufacturing purposes in 1921 about 40,000 quintals of raw cacao and in 1922 38,000 quintals, but this industry has almost no exports. The Government tobacco factories manufacture annually over 100,000 quintals of tobacco, exclusively for home consumption. In 1922 the imports of leaf tobacco were 261,734 quintals.

The annual yield of timber exceeds 10 million cubic meters of which the larger part is soft wood used for fuel, construction, and the manufacture of wood pulp. Hardwood is used for the manufacture of railroad ties, furniture, etc.

EXPORTS (In quintals)

	1920	1921	1922
Firewood	2,331,763	5,653,601	2,345,938
Mine timbers	1,002,761	1,435,229	3,334,763
Pulpwood	639,113	870,944	5,166,499
Construction timber and lumber	4,604,921	5,978,763	11,441,178
Railroad ties	3,958	61,993	61,896

Coal is imported from Germany and Poland, while lignite, briquettes and coke are exported largely to Austria, Hungary, Poland, Rumania and Yugoslavia.

	Imports (in million quintals)			Exports		
	1920	1921	1922	1920	1921	1922
Lignite	0.4	0.2	0.2	33.9	44.4	34.6
Coal	11.3	9.5	5.2	6.9	12.9	10.3
Coke	1.2	1.1	0.9	1.5	3.0	3.5
Briquettes	..	..	..	0.5	1.7	1.4

The output of pig iron is at present very low largely on account of the high price of coke. Consequently, for the manufacture of steel and malleable iron, scrap and imported materials are used to a large extent. In the engineering industry the manufacture of motors of all kinds is important as well as the manufacture of machinery for sugar mills, breweries, and distilleries, and the manufacture of agricultural implements. The development of the electro-technical industry is very promising but the output is insufficient to cover the home needs, and the imports from Germany and Austria are large. The automobile industry, technically perfect, is handicapped by the relatively small market.

FOREIGN TRADE

	Imports	Exports
	1920 (In quintals)	
Iron and steel and manufactures of....	1,147,900	1,639,265
Nonferrous metals and metal wares....	287,022	46,010
Machinery	299,178	403,824
Electric machinery and apparatus......	56,505	11,209
	1921	
Iron and steel and manufactures of....	1,228,481	2,034,806
Nonferrous metals and metal wares....	241,431	70,495
Machinery	254,423	498,116
Electric machinery and apparatus......	64,777	18,069
	1922	
Iron and steel and manufactures of....	2,198,587	1,963,741
Nonferrous metals and metal wares....	262,554	65,892
Machinery	249,503	301,803
Electric machinery and apparatus......	37,585	9,488

VALUE IN MILLIONS OF CZECHOSLOVAK CROWNS

	Imports	Exports
	1920	
Iron and steel and manufactures of.........	930	1,511
Nonferrous metals and metal wares........	766	344
Machinery	560	558
Electric machinery and apparatus..........	769	124
Vehicles	281	53
	1921	
Iron and steel and manufactures of........	541	1,369
Nonferrous metals and metal wares........	526	411
Machinery	544	905
Electric machinery and apparatus..........	753	173
Vehicles	104	52
	1922	
Iron and steel and manufactures of........	430	768
Nonferrous metals and metal wares........	379	243
Machinery	353	294
Electric machinery and apparatus..........	206	64
Vehicles	72	18

The textile industry originated and developed in the former empire which, with a population of 56 million, was a large open market. Even then the textile industry was dependent on exports. It is much more dependent on exports now, when the home market has been reduced to one-fourth its former size and when the industry must seek foreign markets for as much as three-fourths or four-fifths of its production. The manufacture of artificial silk established after the war will make imports unnecessary.

VALUE OF THE IMPORTS AND EXPORTS OF TEXTILE PRODUCTS
(in million Czechoslovak crowns)

	Imports	Exports
	1920	
Cotton and manufactures of cotton	5,030	2,526
Flax, hemp, jute and manufactures of	311	351
Wool and manufactures of wool	2,212	6,684
Silk and manufactures of silk	299	152
Clothing and millinery	591	905
	1921	
Cotton and manufactures of cotton	3,447	3,802
Flax, hemp, jute and manufactures of	507	422
Wool and manufactures of wool	2,125	4,104
Silk and manufactures of silk	476	451
Clothing and millinery	64	793
	1922	
Cotton and manufactures of cotton	1,972	2,566
Flax, hemp, jute and manufactures of	296	374
Wool and manufactures of wool	1,606	2,807
Silk and manufactures of silk	266	204
Clothing and millinery	48	500

The glass industry, having about 400 establishments, some of them of world-wide reputation, has a tradition of many generations. The glass works are located chiefly in the coal regions or in the forests; the glass refineries are scattered through the mountain valleys. The sand needed for the clearest glass is imported from Saxony while the necessary fluxes (sodium carbonate and sulphate, potash) are produced by local industries. The annual production of hollow glass is estimated at 415,000 tons, of window and plate glass at 131,800 tons, and of special glass at 187,000 tons. The value of all the glass manufactured in 1920 was estimated at 1,898 million Czechoslovak crowns, in 1921 at 2,072 million Czechoslovak crowns.

The porcelain industry, concentrated in the vicinity of the watering place of Karlovy Vary (Carlsbad) where kaolin is found and fuel can be obtained from a lignite field nearby, is largely an exporting industry. The value of poreclain and earthenware exported in 1920 was 295 million Czechoslovak crowns and in 1921 488 million Czechoslovak crowns. China clay is also exported to Germany.

The leather industry has about 260 factories capable to work 150,000 cattle hides weekly. The manufacture of leather soles is an old branch of this industry; the manufacture of shoe uppers of chrome leather has also been established. The shoe industry, when fully employed, produces about 40 million pairs of shoes annually and exports three-fourths of its output. The glove industry also has an extensive export trade and old business connections with the western countries. The imports of leather and leather goods in 1920 were valued at 367 million Czechoslovak crowns, and in 1921 at 381 million Czechoslovak crowns; the exports in 1920 amounted to 642 million Czechoslovak crowns, and in 1921 to 862 million Czechoslovak crowns. In 1922 the imports were 126, and the exports 479 million.

The paper industry is working under favorable conditions because it has an abundance of the necessary timber and a great number of factories manufacturing chemical woodpulp. The printing and graphic industries have establishments of world-wide reputation. Both of these branches of industry have a large foreign trade. In 1920 imports of pulp, paper, and paper wares were valued at 226 million Czechoslovak crowns, the exports at 695 million Czechoslovak crowns; in 1921 the imports were 126 million Czechoslovak crowns and the exports 654 million Czechoslovak crowns.

The chemical industry is represented by several large establishments which export sulphuric acid, muriatic acid, calcium carbide, white-lead, glue, etc. Many small establishments manufacture varnishes and paints, pastes, etc. The soap industry is very highly developed as is also the manufacture of fertilizers. The latter now uses annually about 50,000 tons of natural phosphates, but the imports of the finished products are still greater. The trade balance of the chemical industry is rather unfavorable, because the consumption of chemicals in the textile and the leather industries, and of drugs, is large and must be covered by imports, largely from Germany. Mineral oils also must be imported. In a large measure these are imported refined, as the home refineries have difficulties in obtaining crude petroleum from Poland and Rumania. The imports in 1920 were 1,318,315 quintals, in 1921 1,061,020 quintals, in 1922 991,161 quintals.

There is also a large group of special industries, working for the most part for exports. These include the manufacture of pinchbeck jewelry concentrated in the district of the glass industry of Jablonec, the manufacture of buttons, enameled ware, pencils, matches, bent-wood furniture, musical instruments, linen, cravats, hats, laces, and embroidery.

The development of the foreign trade since the establishment of the Republic in 1918 is interesting.

The statistics for the year 1919 were based on the declarations of importers and exporters submitted with the applications for export or import permits. According to these statistics the imports totaled 6,555 million Czechoslovak crowns and the exports 5,323 million Czechoslovak crowns. The unfavorable balance of trade was due to the exhaustion of the country which was almost bare of foodstuffs and of raw materials needed for its industries. Grain and flour were imported to the amount of 1,444 million Czechoslovak crowns; fats for 845 million Czechoslovak crowns; other foodstuffs, beverages, spices, coffee, etc., for 471 million Czechoslovak crowns. The raw materials imported included: cotton for 918 million Czechoslovak crowns, wool for 554 million Czechoslovak crowns, hides for 230 million Czechoslovak crowns. These imports were paid for with the exports of sugar (1,571 million Czechoslovak crowns); wood and coal (614 million Czechoslovak crowns); hops, malt, seeds, etc. (564 million Czechoslovak crowns); glass, iron wares, etc. It is interesting to note that the United States of America held the first place in Czechoslovak imports (1,868 million Czechoslovak crowns); foodstuffs and raw materials for the textile industry were the chief imports. For the same reason the imports from Italy and Switzerland were unusually large. The exports were directed chiefly to Germany and Austria; Vienna, a great distributing center, buys Czechoslovak products largely for re-exports. The western countries bought chiefly Czechoslovak sugar. The statistics of 1919 are not a picture of commerce in its natural continuity. In the first half of the year 1919 Czechoslovakia had only one possibility of shipping its goods and that was by way of Trieste. The first raw materials and semi-manufactured products for the textile industry were bought in Italy, and large purchases were also made from liquidation of war supplies in France. Transportation by the river Labe (Elbe) was not possible until May 1919. It was almost impossible to trade with Rumania and Yugoslavia, as the means of transportation were lacking. The trade with Hungary and Poland was handicapped by political tension. All trade was hampered by a strict system of control of imports and exports and by restrictions imposed on dealing in foreign exchange.

The following two years, 1920 and 1921 were a period of export expansion. The exchange value of the Czechoslovak crown was low, the prices of Czechoslovak products in the world markets were low and attracted foreign buyers, speculators, manufacturers and business men who were tempted by the profits on exchange. The industry renewed its activities when supplies of raw materials were received but there was a shortage of coal at times. The balance of trade for those two years was favorable. The statistics for 1920 and 1921 are based on declarations of the quantity of exported goods, which are submitted to the custom offices. The value of exports is then estimated by the commission of experts composed of manufacturers and business men connected with the State Bureau of Statistics.

FOREIGN TRADE ACCORDING TO QUANTITIES

	Imports tons	Exports tons
1921	3,991,174	9,742,735
1922	3,194,215	9,490,262

FOREIGN TRADE ACCORDING TO VALUE
(in million Czechoslovak crowns)

	Imports	Exports	Excess of exports
1920	23,384	27,569	4,185
1921	22,433	27,311	4,878
1922	12,695	18,086	5,391

In the first half of 1923, Czechoslovakia foreign trade was recovering from the decline sustained in the second half of 1922, when signs of a certain unsteadiness appeared after the sudden rise of the crown which increased the difficulties of trading with countries with depreciated currencies.

Statistics of foreign trade as regards the country of origin and destination are as follows:

	1920			
	Imports		Exports	
	(million quintals)	(million Cecho-slovak crowns)	(million quintals)	(million Czecho-slovak crowns)
Germany	20.8	5,604	30.9	3,330
Austria	3.3	3,042	23.9	9,678
Hungary	0.8	656	3.2	2,512
United States	2.1	4,111	0.2	544
France	0.2	955	1.9	2,374
Poland	1.0	399	1.7	1,425
Italy	0.5	1,003	1.7	1,301
Holland	0.6	1,316	0.6	557
Belgium and Luxemburg	0.8	1,038	0.08	135
United Kingdom	0.3	1,009	0.2	135
Rumania	0.5	308	0.3	732
Yugoslavia	0.3	340	0.6	1,082
Switzerleand	0.1	625	0.9	766

	1921 Imports (million quintals)	Imports (million Czecho-slovak crowns)	Exports (million quintals)	Exports (million Czecho-slovak crowns)
Germany	18.9	5,862	36.2	3,061
Austria	3.2	1,983	33.4	7,835
Hungary	2.5	926	13.3	3,066
United States	3.8	4,547	0.2	771
France	0.3	638	1.7	1,317
Poland	1.4	384	3.6	1,424
Italy	0.8	733	1.4	921
Holland	0.9	1,106	0.8	567
Belgium and Luxemburg	0.4	447	0.3	294
United Kingdom	0.9	1,342	1.5	2,104
Rumania	0.9	482	0.8	1,175
Yugoslavia	0.6	367	1.3	2,008
Switzerland	0.06	316	0.8	520

The largest turnover is shown in the trade with Germany and Austria, and with the States which were formerly part of Austria-Hungary. In trade with Germany, Czechoslovakia has an unfavorable balance due largely to the imports of iron ware, machines, electro-technical articles, chemicals, dyes, drugs, textiles, etc. On the other hand, there is a large favorable balance with Austria resulting from the exports of coal, sugar, textiles, glass, porcelain, etc., largely for re-export. The large unfavorable balance in the trade with America is caused by the purchase of raw materials and foodstuffs. The difference is made up by exports to other countries.

BY QUANTITIES THE CZECHOSLOVAK FOREIGN TRADE WAS DISTRIBUTED AS FOLLOWS:

(per cent)

	Imports 1920	Imports 1921	Imports 1922	Exports 1920	Exports 1921	Exports 1922
Raw materials	78.8	78.5	74.0	80.4	82.6	81.0
Semi-manufactured goods	7.3	6.2	11.1	8.0	7.1	10.7
Manufactures	13.9	15.3	14.9	11.6	10.3	8.3

ACCORDING TO VALUE:						
Raw materials	44.2	53.7	57.1	10.8	14.3	19.1
Semi-manufactured goods	14.3	12.3	13.3	10.9	10.3	17.0
Manufactures	41.5	34.0	29.6	78.3	75.4	63.9

The distribution of the imports and exports of merchandise according to the branches of production is shown in the following table:

	(per cent) Imports	(per cent) Exports
Agricultural and forest products	10.2	10.7
Products of the mines and foundries	68.6	69.7
Industrial products	21.2	19.6

These figures have been calculated according to weight.

All these statistics show that Czechoslovakia is a country of intensive agricultural and industrial production and, to a large extent, an exporting country. The high standard of living makes necessary the importation of large quantities of foreign goods, particularly raw materials and foodstuffs.

The geographical situation of Czechoslovakia in the center of Europe and the fact that the country had been a part of the customs union of Austria-Hungary explain why the trade with foreign countries has not developed in all branches on an independent basis. Prague formerly had an important wholesale trade in coffee and colonial produce but in the customs union of Austria-Hungary this trade was directed to Trieste through differential duties. This trade is now developing very promisingly.

One branch of the textile industry purchases cotton and wool directly on the foreign exchanges. Smaller establishments make their purchases in Bremen. That explains why the American statistics, for example, do not show the total exports of cotton to Czechoslovakia. Metals and other raw materials are in general purchased through wholesale houses (in Berlin, Frankfort, Hamburg). The great American firms furnish daily quotations on copper only to the larger commercial centers of Europe. In many other branches the small concerns prefer to buy in smaller quantities from German wholesale houses as they can easily calculate the purchasing price and cost of transportation. Many exporting industries have their own selling organizations, as the sugar, malt, alcohol, and enamel ware industries. Large establishments dealing in glass, porcelain, chemicals, and textile products, have their own connections and representatives abroad. The export trade of Jablonec negotiates the exports of its products directly to all parts of the world. Several makes of agricultural implements, plows and sowing machines, were popular before the war throughout the Balkans, Russia, and Siberia. Several large establishments of this kind have now formed a united selling organization affiliated with the engineering industry. The iron industry which previously had been in a cartel with the Austrian iron industry now has an independent sales organization. Sometimes foreign buyers come directly to the place of production, as, for instance, in the case of the Zatec hops. In some cases the producers sell the goods to German exporters, especially in Berlin and Hamburg, hops in Nuremberg, etc. The Czechoslovak industry makes large export and import transactions at the Leipzig fair. The textile industries of cotton and silk have their own sales branches and warehouses in Vienna and direct the shipments to the Balkan countries from that city.

It has been the aim, during the last years, to establish our own wholesale houses and to make direct connections in import and export. For the dissemination of trade information and the promotion of direct trade connection, sample fairs have been organized on a larger scale in Prague, in Liberec (here the textile trade is largely represented) and in Bratislava. The Prague Sample Fairs which have been held so far have attracted large numbers of visitors, especially from Yugoslavia and Rumania. For commercial purposes the waterways are also being used, namely the Labe (Elbe) for transportation to Hamburg, and the Danube. The port of Bratislava on the Danube is rapidly becoming a distributing center for trade with the Balkans. The Danube may in the future become an important highway for the importation of grain. Swedish ore for the ironworks in Ostrava-Karvin is transported by way of the Odra (Oder) to the transfer point of Kozli (Kosel). The imports by water amount to about 17 per cent and the exports to 13 per cent of the total trade by weight. The greater part of water-borne traffic is directed by way of the Labe.

Recent statistics show that the Czechoslovak exports to the western countries are steadily increasing. The chief articles of this increasing trade are sugar, timber, glass, porcelain, malt, paper, matches, and machinery. The trade with Hungary, Poland, Rumania and Yugoslavia has temporarily declined because of the appreciation of the Czechoslovak crown. The exports of

Czechoslovak products to the western countries have stimulated also the imports from that part of Europe, as, for example, from France, Netherlands and Switzerland. It appears also that the other succession States of former Austria-Hungary are endeavoring to build up their own industries as their home market, protected by high duties, offers favorable opportunities. The Czechoslovak industries, producing largely for export, will doubtless seek to meet the new conditions by improving the quality of their products and by greater specialization.

IX

THE COMMERCIAL POLICY AND THE TARIFF

Dr. Fr. Peroutka, Division Chief in the Ministry of Commerce

As soon as the new State had been established, October 28, 1918, the transit of goods across the new frontiers of the Czechoslovak Republic was subjected to control, though Czechoslovakia was not organized as an independent customs territory until the passage of the law of February 20, 1919, defining the customs territory and providing for the collection of duties. The old customs frontier was retained as against Germany, while a new frontier line was gradually developed as against Austria, Hungary, and Poland. Under the law of February 20, 1919, duties were to be levied also on goods coming from the other territories of the former Austria-Hungary which had in the past formed a single customs territory with Czechoslovakia. The old organization of the customs service, based on the experience of many decades, was retained.

The duties on goods imported into Czechoslovakia were to be paid in gold, at the old rates fixed by the autonomous tariff of 1906. However, under the law of February 20, 1919, the Minister of Finance was authorized, with the consent of the Ministers of Commerce and of Agriculture, temporarily to reduce or abolish duties on certain classes of necessaries. The goods which were subsequently placed on the free list included grain, flour, seeds, cattle, animal products, fats, and various raw materials, such as minerals, carving materials, tanning materials, gums and resins, crude mineral oils, etc. The old prewar rates were retained for semi-manufactured articles and certain other needed commodities. In the case of other goods the prewar rates were increased by an exchange surtax amounting to 200 per cent, excepting only articles of luxury (the duties on which the Minister of Finance might have collected in francs) for which the surtax was fixed at 220 per cent. Inasmuch as the currency of Czechoslovakia then naturally stood far below its gold parity and its exchange value declined still further in the course of the years 1919 and 1920, it will be easily seen that, in comparison with prewar conditions, tariff protection had been largely reduced.

In those days, however, all imports and exports were partially and still are controlled through a system of permits. No goods could cross the frontier except under a special permit issued by the Czechoslovak Import and Export Commission organized under an ordinance of the Ministry of Commerce of November 22, 1918.

In the early days following the armistice the new State, like the rest of central Europe, was almost bare of foodstuffs, raw materials, and other commodities. By prohibition against exportation sufficient supplies of necessaries were to be assured to the people. Hence the Commission would forbid the exportation of foodstuffs and raw materials, control the exportation of coal, and permit the exportation of other goods only in case the people were assured a sufficient supply at reasonable prices. The imports were likewise regulated; the Commission would, for example, seek to restrain the importation of oranges, wines, and other luxuries, as well as of goods which were already obtainable in the domestic market. These measures were intended also to protect the currency. In addition to the Import and Export Commission, a Central Exchange Bureau was established. The exporters were required to turn over to the Bureau all foreign exchange obtained for goods sold abroad, and the Bureau would reassign such exchange for the purchase of foodstuffs and important raw materials or such other goods for which import permits could be obtained.

The authority of the Import and Export Commission was somewhat modified in the course of time. By an ordinance of February 26, 1919, some of its rights and duties were transferred to industrial syndicates. The intention was to permit the several branches of industry and trade to manage their own affairs. It seemed also that such associations would be in a better position than individual firms when purchasing raw materials abroad or selling domestic goods or supplying materials and machinery for the devastated regions, since in such cases the financing would be beyond the means of individual firms or corporations. It soon became evident, however, that if trade was to be thus controlled at all an impartial Government bureau should be given preference over groups of interested parties that might have to pass on applications of their competitors. As a matter of fact, no large transactions were ever effected for the joint account of the syndicates. In a few cases, in addition to the syndicates which possessed official authority, special associations were organized, as, for example, for the purchase of cotton, of fats for the manufacture of soap, and for the importation of mineral oils. Such transactions, however, caused considerable difficulties to both industry and the State later on, as the distribution and liquidation of the stocks so purchased had to be carried out at a time when the world prices had already fallen while the exchange value of the Czechoslovak crown had risen. The syndicates were consequently divested of their official authority, and the control of the foreign trade was reorganized and intrusted to a special Foreign Trade Bureau established under the law of June 24, 1920. The Bureau revised the system of permits, issued lists of goods which might be exported freely, adopted more liberal rules for the granting of import permits, and co-operated in the modification of the control of foreign exchange.

Foreign trade continues under partial control, at the time of writing. The control is criticized by many as troublesome, but it has been demanded by producers in many cases and by consumers in others. It was found to be necessary particularly in 1919 and 1920 when Czechoslovak exchange was falling, and it was necessary to protect the crown against further depreciation through payments for unprofitable imports and to prevent a precipitate selling out of the domestic stocks for the sake of the delusive profits to be made on exchange. The State made an attempt to obtain for the Treasury a part of the exchange profits by imposing export duties on hops, malt, lumber, spirits, etc. The proceeds were disappointing, however. It has also been charged that State control of the sugar exports had made it impossible for the trade to take advantage of the high prices of sugar in the world market.

If the control of imports is to be judged fairly the low rates of duties must be taken into consideration. In the system originally adopted in Czechoslovakia low import duties were combined with the restriction of imports by permits. Domestic production was to be protected by prohibitions against importation. When importation was to be permitted for any special reason it would have been inconsistent, under the existing economic conditions, to place on the consumer an additional burden in the form of high import duties.

That the system of trade control has been maintained in Czechoslovakia so long has been largely due to the existence of similar conditions in the neighboring States. In Germany, under the so-called "Planwirtschaft," a complicated system of import and export control was elaborated which made similar measures necessary in Czechoslovakia also. Austria likewise made use of import and export prohibition. In Hungary a similar system of control has recently been reinforced by strict provisions relating to foreign exchange. Switzerland also considers the regulation of imports as indispensable in certain lines. Rumania and Yugoslavia have passed through many and varied phases of a similar system. The original causes leading to the adoption of the system have largely disappeared both in Czechoslovakia and in the neighboring countries, but the system has been of good service to Czechslovak industry, particularly so in times of sudden fluctuations of exchange (collapse of the German mark, for example) when odious anti-dumping laws might otherwise have been necessary. The question of trade control was considered by the delegates of the succession States at the Portorose conference toward the end of 1921, and the removal of trade restrictions was recommended under certain conditions which have not been fulfilled, however. The Czechoslovak Government showed its willingness to suppress that system when it abolished the independent Foreign Trade Bureau by the law of January 19, 1922. The work of the Bureau, reduced to about one-fourth of its former extent, was transferred to a division of the Ministry of Commerce.

This system of foreign trade control in Central European States explains why the earliest Czechoslovak treaties with other States were "compensation" treaties providing for the exchange of specified goods. By the treaty with Austria of March 12, 1919, Czechoslovakia obtained freedom of transit to and from the port of Trieste, and the liquidation of various war supplies remaining in Vienna, such as metals, hides, textiles and demobilization materials, as well as supplies of certain industrial materials found in Austria in abundance, such as magnesite for the metal industry and tanning materials for the leather industry. In return, Czechoslovakia agreed to supply Austria with coal and that at a time when, under the postwar disorganization of mining, the Czechoslovak industries themselves were suffering from a shortage of coal. Austria was also to receive a large quantity of Czechoslovak sugar at the price of 3.20 Cz. crowns per kilogram for household use and 5.40 Cz. crowns per kilogram for industrial uses, and the sugar was delivered at a time when the world price had risen to 20-30 Cz. crowns per kilogram. The treaties with Poland and Rumania secured to Czechoslovakia supplies of crude and refined mineral oils in return for metal wares, machinery, and other industrial products. The treaty with Yugoslavia was to secure to Czechoslovakia supplies of grain and cattle in return for sugar and industrial products of various kinds. In the early times, however, trade with these countries suffered greatly from the difficulties of transportation; in 1920, for example, it was cheaper to bring grain and flour to Czechoslovakia from America than from these nearby States.

The earliest Czechoslovak treaties with Germany provided for the delivery of Czechoslovak lignite to Germany in return for coal, and for the removal of certain import and export prohibitions by both parties. The general commercial treaty with Germany, signed June 29, 1920, at Prague, provides for the most-favored-nation treatment in matters of trade as well as in regard to the carrying on of industry or trade by the citizens of either State in the territory of the other. The treaty also modifies various import and export restrictions of both countries.

The Czechoslovak import restrictions were further

relaxed by treaties with the western States, notedly with France and Italy. The treaty of November 25, 1920, permitted the importation from France of large quantities of wine, silks, woolen fabrics, clothing and millinery articles, rubber and leather goods, automobiles, toilet soaps, and perfumeries, and made free the importation of numerous articles of produce, raw materials, metal and chemical goods. In return, France would apply the rates of its minimum tariff to certain Czechoslovak goods or reduce the rates of the general tariff. The treaty with Italy, concluded March 23, 1921, authorized the importation of certain quantities of automobiles, tires, rubber goods, soaps, silks, hats, wine, oranges, lemons, figs, and other products, from Italy. In return, Czechoslovakia obtained the most-favored-nation treatment in matters of the tariff and a modification of certain import restrictions then in force in Italy. In all other respects the treaties with France and Italy as well as the treaty of April 23, 1921, with Rumania, the treaty of October 20, 1921, with Poland, and the treaty of October 7, 1922, with Latvia, follow the tenor and the methods of prewar treaties. The Czechoslovak treaty of November 19, 1921, with Spain resembles the treaties with France and Italy.

Neither the commercial treaties mentioned above nor the negotiations carried on with the United Kingdom, Belgium, the Netherlands, Denmark, Greece, Portugal, and Japan, contain any special provisions affecting the Czechoslovak tariff rates. The Czechoslovak tariff thus remains an autonomous tariff. The most-favored-nation clause contained in all the treaties will, therefore, remain inoperative for some time as regards import duties. It is easy to see why negotiations in regard to rates have not been commenced. Owing to the fluctuations of exchange, the tariff rates of the neighboring countries of Germany, Austria, Poland, and Hungary, whose trade relations with Czechoslovakia are very active, are even less stable than those of Czechoslovakia. In the treaties with France and Italy which, under other conditions, might have affected the tariff rates, the interest was centered in import permits. Other States, such as the Netherlands, Belgium, Denmark, or the United Kingdom, have no reasons to give up their tariff autonomy in treaties with other States and consequently are not concerned about tariff rates.

The rates of the autonomous tariff of Czechoslovakia were revised several times in 1920 and 1921.

By the ordinance of May 21, 1921, the system of exchange surtaxes, modelled on the French postwar tariff, was adopted. The rate of duty is established by multiplying the basic (nominal) rate with the proper coefficient. Varying coefficients were assigned to the several items of the tariff. Articles of luxury and articles specially protected were given co-efficients 10 to 16. Semi-manufactured articles and goods with lower protection received the coefficient of 7. Where importation of goods was to be made easier, the coefficients were 1 to 5.

When Czechoslovak exchange began to improve toward the end of 1921 while the German mark was falling it became necessary to revise the tariff rates for the protection of Czechoslovak industry against the competition of Germany and other neighboring States with depreciated currencies. The revision was carried out by the ordinance of December 18, 1921, going into effect January 1, 1922. The coefficients for manufactured goods averaged 10 to 15, increasing to 20 to 30 in a few cases of goods specially protected. In the first half of 1922 when the Czechoslovak crown was quoted in Zurich at about 10 centimes or nearly one-tenth of its prewar value, the protection of Czechoslovak industry was increased by the revision one-half or even doubled (in rare cases, trebled) as compared with prewar rates.

A new upward movement of the Czechoslovak crown commencing in July, 1922, raised its value in Zurich to 18 centimes in October of 1922. By that time the German mark had fallen in value to 0.01 Cz. crown. The effect of those violent changes was two-fold. Czechoslovakia was enabled to purchase raw materials abroad at a lower cost, e. g., cotton, wool, copper, hides, rubber, as well as cereals, flour, cattle, and meats. On the other hand, the level of prices prevailing in Czechoslovakia until the summer of 1921 was abnormally high, particularly in comparison with the prices in Germany and Austria. The consumers were clamoring for lower prices while the producers were still afraid of German competition during the period of transition. However, the upward course of the crown brought about an energetic movement for the lowering of prices in Czechoslovakia, and the movement was supported by the Government through the reduction of certain taxes (such as the taxes on coal and coke) which had contributed to increase the cost of production. In new negotiations between the manufacturers and organized labor wages were reduced 20 to 30 per cent; the new wage agreement concluded with the coal miners in October of 1922 particularly was expected to produce far reaching results. The prices were likewise to be lowered by a reduction of tariff rates announced by the Government in a proclamation issued September 9, 1922. The new revision of tariff co-efficients prepared in agreement with the Chambers of Commerce and Industry will reduce the import duties in many cases by as much as one-fourth. Czechoslovakia, it would seem, will thus be the first State to adopt, in its tariff policy, a course that is a direct opposite of the course followed in recent years by nearly all the countries of the world.

In the tariff policy of Czechoslovakia there still remains one problem which demands solution. As a result of the war and the difficulties of obtaining supplies after the armistice the import duties on grain and flour have been suspended and the duties on cattle, meats and fats reduced to a minimum. Czechoslovakia, however, has a large and progressive agricultural population which now demands protection for its produce as a matter of natural right. It is easy to understand the clamor for grain duties at a time when the world prices of grain have declined so markedly between April and October of 1922 while the purchasing power of the crown abroad has nearly doubled. The solution of this problem has been deferred until the next session of Parliament when the new autonomous tariff is to be considered.

X

RAILWAYS

Dr. Václav Burger, late Minister of Railways

In Czechoslovakia the railways are owned partly by the State and partly by private corporations, and are operated, for the most part, by the State. The length of the lines open for traffic at the end of 1921 is shown in the following table (in kilometers):

Equipped with	Operated by State: State owned	Operated by State: Privately owned	Operated privately	Operated by foreign States: State owned	Operated by foreign States: Privately owned	Operated by foreign States: Foreign railways	Total length, km.
Steam locomotives	7,792	3,826	1,150	41	5	97	12,913
Electric locomotives	..	51	98	..	..	..	150

The State railways are directed by the Ministry of Railways and managed by seven district bureaus of the State Railway Adminstration. The Ministry of Railways is invested with absolute power to direct all railway traffic and to control the adminstration of the State railways as well as of the private lines. The Ministry is divided into 7 sections: (1) Minister's Office, (2) Judicial and Administrative, (3) Financial, (4) Commercial, (5) Construction, (6) Machinery and Shops, (7) Traffic. The district bureaus are located in Prague, Plzeň, Hradec Králové, Brno, Olomouc, Bratislava and Košice. Under the direction of the

Ministry of Railways and in accordance with its plans and rules, these bureaus have charge of the local administration of all railway lines within their territories. They are responsible for the security, order and regularity of traffic. At the head of each bureau is a director with one or two assistant directors.

The mileage of the railways in the several districts is shown below:

District bureau:	Length of line		
Prague	1,895 km.	or	1,178 miles
Plzeň	2,027 km.	or	1,260 miles
Hradec Král	2,014 km.	or	1,251 miles
Brno	1,256 km.	or	781 miles
Olomouc	1,741 km.	or	1,081 miles
Bratislava	2,147 km.	or	1,334 miles
Košice	1,614 km.	or	1,003 miles

(including Košice-Bohumin line.)

The total length of State and private lines operated by the State is 12,694 km, out of which 953 km are double-tracked.

Railway stations operating local traffic directly, and the construction and other services, are under the jurisdiction of the district bureaus. The following table shows the number of these offices:

District bureau	Traffic administration	Maintenance sections	Locomotive sheds	Stations and traffic offices	Workshops	Sign shops	Warehouses
Prague	4	17	11	384	3	1	3
Plzeň	5	14	7	333	4	1	1
Hradec Král	3	20	9	387	3	2	2
Brno	2	12	7	322	1	1	1
Olomouc	.	17	5	228	3	1	3
Bratislava	.	17	2	304	1	1	2
Koštice	.	6	2	81	1	1	1
Total	14	103	46	2,040	16	8	13

The chief private railways in the Czechoslovak Republic are:

1. The Ustí-Teplice Railway	253 km.	or	157 miles
2. The Buštěhrad Railway	422 km.	or	263 miles
3. Local railways	293 km.	or	182 miles
Total private railways (with the exception of the Košice-Bohumín line)	968 km.	or	602 miles
Lines with double tracks	441 km.	or	274 miles

The Košice-Bohumín Railway and most of the local railways are under the State Administration.

The Czechoslovak Railways are, with some exceptions, steam railways of a normal gauge of 1,435 mm. The characteristic standards of line construction as to weight of rail, grades, and curves are as follows:

Railway line:	Smallest radius of curve (meters)	Steepest grade (1:1000)	Weight of rail kg. per 1 meter
Cheb-Plzeň-Praha-Č. Třebová-Olomouc-Bohumín-Žilina-Košice	300	11	35.6
Podmokly-Praha-C. Budějovice-H. Dvořiště	300	11	35.6
Č. Třebová-Brno-Břeclava-Bratislava	230	7.9	35.6
Bratislava-Žilina	300	7.5	42.8
Bratislava-Parkáň Nána	600	4	42.8
Plzeň-Brod n.-L.	350	10	35.6
Plzeň-Duchcov	250	13	35.6
Plzeň--Č. Budějovice-Cmunt	300	11	35.6
Praha-Most	250	16.7	35.6
Teplice-Podmokli	200	20	35.6
Louny-Zdice-Protivin	250	15.5	35.6
Praha-Hradec Kraál.-Mezilesí	250	15.5	25.6
Praha-Všetaty-Rumburk	280	17	35.6
Šatov-Děčín	250	10	35.6
Choceň-Mezimostí	284	14.3	35.6
Brno-Přerov	400	6.7	35.6
Olomouc-Opava	225	17	35.6
Brno-Vláry Pass-Teplá	250	16	33
Bratislava-Komárno	250	5	23.6
Other lines	180	25	35.6
Local railways	150-180	25-40	26

The table shows that the Czechoslovak lines are not of a uniform type. This is explained by the origin of the system which has been formed gradually by the acquisition of various private lines. The Czechoslovak administration plans in time to strengthen the permanent way and the bridges to such a degree as to increase the maximum admissible wheel load of locomotives, which is at present only 14.5 tons, to 20 tons for the trunk lines and to 16 tons for the secondary lines. It plans to increase the maximum speed of trains which now varies between 80 and 90 km, and on the Slovak lines only 60 or 70 km per hour, to 120 km per hour. About 5,000 km of rails will have to be reinforced, and at least 310 km of rails will have to be renewed annually in order to increase the speed of trains on lines of international traffic to 100-120 km.

The Condition of the Lines After the War.

The railways of Czechoslovakia—with the exception of some lines in the eastern part of Slovakia and Carpathian Russia—were not damaged by military operations during the war; it was only the invasion of the Magyar bolshevik troops into Slovak territory in the year 1919 that caused considerable damage. The railways suffered, however, during the war by the insufficient maintenance of the lines when all sections of the railway system were unusually overtaxed. Under the Austrian and Hungarian administration little attention was paid to the needs of the Czechoslovak territories, and nothing was done to improve the means of communication between Slovakia in the east and Bohemia in the west. After the Revolution it became necessary to equip the lines for the traffic from east to west along the long axis of the Republic. As there were comparatively few railways running in that direction and, moreover, those were of weak construction, it was necessary to reinforce and supplement the existing lines.

In order to secure the communication between Prague, the capital, and Bratislava, the most important river port of the Czechoslovak Republic on the Danube, the Břeclava-Bratislava line had to be strengthened and double-tracked. The second tracks of the lines Česká Třebová-Olomouc, Prague-Plzeň, as well as the second tracks of other lines in Bohemia are being constructed to a total length of 112 km.

By the readjustment of frontiers, particularly in Slovakia, some lines have been cut off from the railway system. By the construction of the connecting line near Banrieve the separated lines in the district of Gemer have again been connected with the system. The connection with the Ruthenian territory has been improved by the construction of the Bánovce-Vajany line (19 km), finished in October 1920.

On the Czecho-Austrian and Czecho-Hungarian frontiers there are more than 30 transit stations fitted out very inadequately. These stations are to be fitted out gradually for their new duties. By various provisional constructions the first difficulty has been to a great extent overcome and the definite construction of those stations is now in progress.

Beside the above-mentioned urgent works it was also necessary to prepare a program of systematic improvement and extension of the railway system. By the law of March 30, 1920, the National Assembly adopted a progam for several years and provided 6½ billion crowns for railway construction.

Under this program a direct communication between the eastern and the western parts of the Republic will be accomplished by a new line running from Veselí on the Morava River through the center of Slovakia to Košice-Užhorod-Mukač-Hust. The Czechoslovak railway system will be adapted to the new traffic requirements and will be equipped in such a way as to meet the needs of the expected economic development of the country in the future. The program contemplates the construction of 15 new lines of a total length of 568 km, including 389 km of line in Slovakia and 115 km of connecting lines between Slovakia and the other provinces of the Republic.

In addition, second tracks will be laid on many other lines, and after the completion of this p ogram 16 per cent of the lines in the Republic will be double-tracked. All stations of any importance will be properly reconstructed and fitted out for intensive traffic. At important centers of traffic, especially at Prague, Čes, Tŕebová, Brno, Plzeň, Čes. Budéjovice, Hradec Králové, Bŕeclava, Bratislava and Košice adequate switching yards and sorting depots will be constructed. The preparatory work has so far advanced that it will be possible to begin the construction of all lines in a very short time. For the management of these new constructions three technical departments have been established, at Myjava, Handlová, and Zvoleň.

A special department studies the problem of the reconstruction of the Prague railway stations. The principal problems are: the separation of the passenger from the freight traffic, the separation of the freight traffic from the service of making up trains, and of the local from the through traffic.

In Prague the Wilson Station will be used for the passenger through traffic, and the Masaryk Station for the local traffic. A new switching yard is planned for the making up of passenger trains in both central stations, and a new central freight depot for the freight service. All suburban stations of Prague which are to be adapted for the metropolitan traffic by separating the passenger from the freight traffic will be connected with the switching yards by lines serving the local freight traffic.

To prevent intersection of the through freight traffic with the local freight traffic and to divert the through freight traffic form the center of Prague new local connections will be established. The through freights will encircle Prague over the new belt railway lines. The general projects elaborated on those principles by the research department mentioned above are now being considered by a commission on which all the interested parties are represented. In studying these problems due note is taken of the projected electrification of all railway lines in the environs of Prague within a radius of about 50 km. This problem is to be solved in connection with the electrification of the country which will be accomplished partly by the development of water power and partly by the use of coal.

The construction of local lines to supplement the railway lines has been decreed by the law of June 27, 1919, in force January 1, 1922. Under this law investigations have been made in 130 cases regarding lines of a total length of about 3,000 km, and a program for the construction of local railways in the Czechoslovak Republic will be worked out on the basis of these researches.

Cars

Under article 318 of the Peace Treaty of St. Germain the rolling stock of the Austrian railways was to be distributed by the Reparation Commission in Vienna under the presidency of Sir Francis Dent. This Commission has not yet finished its work.

The number of cars in the territory of the Czechoslovak Republic is much less than the number which would belong to the Czechslovak Republic according to the conditions of traffic during the war. After the Revolution, the rolling stock of Czechoslovakia was short more than 1,890 locomotives and more than 65,000 cars. Since that time the Administration of the State railways has enlarged its rolling stock by the construction of new locomotives and cars, and has for this purpose placed considerable orders both with domestic and foreign manufacturers.

Czechoslovakia obtained 92 locomotives out of the number delivered to the United States of America by Germany, in accordance with the conditions of the armistice. More than 200 locomotives have been delivered by domestic and foreign manufacturers, and more than 300 have ultimately been acquired in the distribution under the Peace Treaty, or from other sources.

The number of locomotives on the main lines in Czechoslovakia is shown in the following table:

	Express and passenger train locomotives	Freight train locomotives	Smaller locomotives	Total
Czechoslovak State railways	939	1,918	770	3,627
Košice-Bohumín railway ...	40	176	57	273
Buštéhrad railway	60	154	23	237
Ustí-Teplice railway	25	113	5	143

The number of locomotives is insufficient for the present demands of traffic, and the needs of traffic will greatly increase with the economic development of the country. Czechoslovakia expects a considerable share from the division of the rolling stock of former Austria-Hungary, but in the meantime, continues to enlarge its own stock of locomotives by other means.

The number of cars in Czechoslovakia according to the census of September 12, 1920, was as follows:

	Passenger cars	Service and mail cars	Freight cars	Covered coal cars	Other cars	Total freight cars	Grand total
Cars of former Austrian railways (St. B.)....	5,407	1,591	5,575	20,689	7,703	33,967	40,965
Cars of former Hungarian railways (M.A.V.)...	708	214	1,926	8,291	1,147	11,374	12,286
Czechoslovak cars (CSD)	1,077	325	8,834	10,822	796	20,452	21,854
Cars of private Czechoslovak railways	732	260	1,348	15,325	1,422	18,095	19,087
Foreign cars	165	8	2,140	9,281	464	11,885	12,058
Total	8,089	2,398	19,823	64,408	11,532	95,763	106,250

Since that census the number of the cars of the Czechoslovak State railways, constructed in domestic factories and marked C. S. D., has increased to 30,000.

The Maintenance of Rolling Stock

After the great war the proportion of locomotives under repair was unusually large (40 per cent against 18 per cent in prewar time). However, with the aid of private industry, and especially by intensive work and the enlargement of our own railway shops, it was possible by the 1st of July, 1921, to reduce the proportion of locomotives under repair to less than 20 per cent.

The maintenance of cars has also improved considerably. At the beginning of 1919 the proportion of passenger cars under repair was 33 per cent, and of freight cars, 14 per cent. At the end of 1920 this percentage decreased to 14.4 for the passenger cars and 7.8 for the freight cars.

In the ten main shops with 10,000 workmen and the 16 locomotive shops with 4,300 workmen, there were repaired:

	In 1920	In the first half of 1921
a. Locomotives:		
Heavy repairs	645	*352
Medium repairs	1,797	923
Light repairs	18,673	10,765
Total locomotives repaired	21,115	12,040
b. Passenger, service and postal cars:		
Heavy repairs	3,305	3,014
Medium repairs	5,370	4,955
Light repairs	48,949	27,292
Total passenger, etc., cars repaired	57,624	36,261
c. Freight cars:		
Heavy repairs	15,164	11,097
Medium repairs	19,915	24,224
Light repairs	288,895	131,013
Total freight cars repaired	323,874	166,334

*Incl. Kos-Boh. railway.

These figures show that the efficiency of the repair shops has improved. Nevertheless, the present capacity of the shops is not adequate for the number of cars which the Czechoslovak State railways will place in service in the near future. It will, therefore, be necessary to build three new main shops for the repairing of cars and to equip the locomotive shops for all light and medium repairs.

The enlargement of the shops was already provided for in the construction and investment program under the law of March 30, 1920. By the intensive work done in the railway shops of the Czechoslovak Republic the rolling stock of the former Austrian and Hungarian State railways was kept in condition for service, and railway traffic in central Europe was saved from disorganization and a possible collapse.

Passenger Traffic

After the war is was necessary to adapt the passenger and the freight traffic to the requirements of the liberated country. By the time-table of June 1920 the internal traffic was essentially improved, especially the connection with Slovakia, and in July 1921 a new time-table was introduced closely approaching the normal conditions and meeting the most important needs of the population. The international passenger traffic was also greatly improved. Prague has a direct connection with Paris via South Germany, with Milan and Rome through Munich, with Belgrade and Trieste through Maribor, with Bucharest through Košice and Királyháza, and with Breslau through Kladsko.

The direct communication Berlin-Vienna over

Děčín-Prague necessitates as yet a change of cars at Děčín, but this difficulty will soon be removed. The passenger traffic carried at present by the Czechoslovak State railways per 1 km. of line is 104 per cent greater than before the war. The intensity of the passenger traffic in comparison with the Austrian prewar conditions is indicated in the following table:

	No. of passengers carried	Per 1 km. of the line	Passengers carried 1 km.	Average journey per passenger km.	Length of line, km.
Austrian State railways in 1913	153,518,550	10,968	5,804,066,266	37.81	14,029
Czechoslovak State railways in 1919	126,463,304	16,731	5,231,868,163	41.37	7,558
Czechoslovak State railways in 1920	174,107,907	22,424	6,869,805,389	39.46	7,892

Freight Traffic

The development of the freight traffic has suffered from a shortage of cars. Therefore the greatest possible care has been given to the organization of through traffic in order to utilize the cars to the utmost. And we have really succeeded in speeding up considerably the circulation of cars (time reduced from 13 to 10 days) and thus at least to some degree satisfied the needs of commerce and industry. Thus, for example, in 1920 from January to November 105,000 more cars were loaded and transported than in the same period in 1919. In spite of this, the movement of freight is far short of the prewar intensity as will be seen from a comparison of the conditions in 1919 with those of 1913, in the following table:

	Fast freight	Parcels	Carload lots	Total
	(in metric tons)			
Austrian state railways in 1913...	1,140,788	5,554,610	79,131,586	85,826,964
Czechoslovak State railways in 1919	326,666	1,643,235	31,582,293	33,357,194
Czechoslovak State railways in 1920	351,449	1,767,886	38,128,098	40,248,033
	(in ton kilometers)			
Austrian State railways in 1913...	148,095,884	809,356,040	11,352,112,402	12,309,564,326
Czechoslovak State railways in 1919	34,765,741	156,552,272	3,272,795,673	3,464,113,686
Czechoslovak State railways in 1920	40,062,484	216,561,724	3,941,392,711	4,198,016,919

	Per 1 km. of the line	Administration shipments	Grand total	Per 1 km. of the line
	(in metric tons)			
Austrian State railways in 1913....	6,118	7,452,801	93,279,765	6,649
Czechoslovak State railways in 1919.	4,177	3,877,004	37,234,198	4,660
Czechoslovak State railways in 1920	5,101	4,603,484	44,851,517	5,686
	(in ton kilometers)			
Austrian State railways in 1913....	870,030	1,228,108,352	13,537,672,678	957,712
Czechoslovak State railways in 1919.	451,031	545,416,690	4,009,530,376	522,044
Czechoslovak State railways in 1920.	532,100	659,223,143	4,857,240,062	615,657

Czechoslovakia is the second country in Europe in sugar production (Germany 2.7, Czechoslovakia 1.9, France 0.9, Netherlands 0.3, Belgium 0.3 millions of tons yearly). Consequently the sugar campaign from the end of September to November is a very difficult period for the Czechoslovak railways, the more so, as it is necessary at the same time to supply the cities with foodstuffs and the industries with coal for winter.

The following table shows the intensity of the traffic resulting from the movement of the sugar crop:

	No. of tons carried		No. of cars used	
	1919	1920	1919	1920
Beets	1,544,421	1,750,462	127,082	125,282
Beet pulp	871,676	1,087,885	67,661	77,928
Raw sugar	189,699	246,601	14,551	17,450
Total	2,605,696	3,080,948	209,294	220,660

The carrying capacity of the cars was increased from 12 to 13.9 tons and the sugar industry supplied 1,000 of its own cars of 20 tons. Owing to a better traffic organization the movement of the sugar crop, which had been attended with some difficulties in 1919, had an entirely normal course in 1920.

Tariffs

In the first period after the revolution, in order to avoid violent economic disturbances, it was necessary to keep in force the rules and tariffs of the Austrian and Hungarian State railways, modifying them only with regard to the new situation. A revision of these tariffs is now being considered.

For international traffic there was at first no legal basis; Czechoslovakia, a new State, was not a member of the Berne Convention for the international railway traffic, and the Czechoslovak Republic had declared that it was not a member of the Union of the German railways. Consequently, it was necessary to conclude preliminary tariff agreements with the railway administrations of the neighboring countries. The agreements were based on the Berne Convention, with some exceptions as required by the situation created after the war. In 1921 the Czechoslovak Republic formally joined the Berne Convention in the sense of the peace treaty. On the 10th of March, 1919, the monetary union of the former Austro-Hungarian territories came to an end. For this reason all the joint tariffs had to be abolished, and temporary agreements had to be negotiated with the neighboring railway administrations of the adjoining countries in order to make possible direct shipments on a single bill of lading.

Tariff agreements for the transportation of passengers and goods have been concluded with the following countries: France, Belgium, England, Germany, Netherlands, Italy, Austria, Yugoslavia, Poland, Rumania, and Hungary.

Unsettled political, economic and currency conditions still make necessary certain special measures concerning import duties and passports at some transit points on the frontier. The situation in this regard is improving, and the respective administrations take care that the inspection is made as quickly as possible without trouble for the travelling public. The transportation of goods is regulated by the agreements with Germany, Belgium, Netherlands, Luxemburg, Denmark, Norway, Poland, Rumania, Yugoslavia, Italy and France.

The international relations will be further consolidated by commercial agreements. Commercial treaties have already been concluded with several countries. The Czechoslovak railway administration seeks to make arrangements with the foreign administrations for a direct dispatch of goods.

Through tariffs have been agreed on for the traffic with Trieste, negotiations for direct tariffs with the ports of the North Sea and the Baltic are in progress. By means of advantageous tariffs the railway administration of Czechoslovakia seeks to promote navigation on the waterways of the Elbe, the Vltava, and the Danube.

In the inland traffic, as we mentioned at the beginning, after the Revolution the Austrian tariffs were applied in Bohemia, Moravia and Silesia, the Hungarian tariffs in Slovakia and Carpathian Ruthenia. On account of the deficit of the Czechoslovak railways, the rates were twice raised in order to achieve at least a partial balance between the value of the goods carried and the rates charged.

With regard to the elongated geographical form of the Czechoslovak Republic, it was very important to connect the eastern provinces, Slovakia and Carpathian Ruthenia, with the Bohemian countries. Special efforts were made to provide direct railway connections with advantageous tariffs and rates for the traffic between the western and the eastern parts of the Republic. Accordingly the rates of the new passenger tariffs are based on a sliding scale, declining in proportion to the increase of the distance. The rates of the private railway line of Košice-Bohumín are calculated in a similar way.

For social reasons, the advantages of reduced fares heretofore granted to manual workers for the journey from their homes to their working places has been extended to the intellectual workers also. For a distance of 150 km. all workers are now entitled to a reduction of 74 to 80 per cent from the regular fare.

A new method of calculation has likewise been introduced in the new tariff for the local transportation of goods on the basis of the total distance between the stations of the Czechoslovak State railways in Bohemia, Moravia, Silesia and Hlučínsko on the one hand and the stations of the Czechoslovak State railways in western and central Slovakia south of Vrutky and Žilina on the other; the same with regard to all local railways operated by the State in Bohemia, Moravia and Silesia. In Slovakia and Carpathian Ruthenia tariffs already in force in Bohemia, Moravia and Silesia have been introduced so that now the same rates are appled in all Czechoslovak territories.

Financial Situation

The figures quoted above show the precarious condition of the Czechoslovak railways at the time when they were taken over by the new administration, and indicate the efforts necessary to maintain and improve the operation of the railways under the disastrous conditions existing after the war. These conditions naturally reacted on the financial situation of the Czechoslovak railways.

The financial depreciation of the former Austrian railways during the war was clearly shown in the fact that the interest earned on the capital invested, which before the war had been 3 per cent, declined to 0.87 per cent for the fiscal year 1914-15, and to 0.17 per cent for 1916-17. In 1917-18 there was a deficit of 110 million crowns, the charges for military transports being calculated as receipts although never paid.

Thus the Czechoslovak Republic inherited a network of railways which was a liability rather than an asset.

On the other hand it was necessary immediately to undertake expensive constructions and investments, if operation was to be maintained and by degrees raised to a decent level. It was likewise indispensable to increase the income of the personnel exhausted by the war and living under wretched conditions. The Czechoslovak State railway budget is consequently burdened with heavy expenditures which are a direct result of the war, i. e., investments made necessary by the reckless exploitation of the system of railways during the war, and the increase of the income of the employees.

When the extraordinary wear and tear caused by the war has been repaired, and the Czechoslovak railway system adapted to the new economic needs, the financial situation of the Czechoslovak State railways may be expected to improve considerably.

XI

THE POSTAL SERVICE

(By the Czechoslovak Ministry of Posts and Telegraphs)

Immediately after the proclamation of the independence of Czechoslovakia, the administration of the posts, telegraphs and telephones took steps to organize the service in accordance with the new conditions. This task was not an easy one, for it meant the reorganization of the old system and the establishment of a new central administration which would have jurisdiction over all the postal, telephone and telegraph communications.

By the law of November 13, 1918, a Ministry of Posts and Telegraphs was established. The Ministry has direct control over six district bureaus of posts and telegraphs—in Prague, Pardubice, Brno, Opava, Bratislava and Košice. The Košice bureau is in charge of the branch office in Beregsas. The district bureaus have supervision over the postal and telegraph offices, building offices and of postal bus transportation. The postal checking bureau is under the direct supervision of the Ministry.

Immediately after its establishment, the Ministry had control over the postal districts of Prague and

Brno only; in Silesia and Slovakia the unsettled political situation made it impossible for the Ministry to take over the postal administration immediately. After the situation became more settled the Ministry took over the district bureau of posts and telegraphs in Opava (Silesia) and in January 1919 the postal and telegraph offices in Slovakia.

In April 1919 a postal and telegraph district bureau was established in Pardubice. The invasion of Slovakia by the Magyar bolsheviks in May 1919 considerably hampered and delayed the reorganization of postal service in Slovakia. However, when the conditions in Slovakia settled down in July 1919, the Ministry established a postal and telegraph district bureau in Bratislava, later also in Košice. In December 1919 a district bureau for the region of Ruthenia was opened in Užhorod. This Užhorod bureau has been closed, and a branch bureau opened in Bergsas.

When the question of Teschen was settled in 1920 the postal service was organized in that part of Silesia also. From the Prussian postal administration the Czechoslovak administration has taken over the post offices in Hlučínsko, and from Austria the offices in the regions of Valčice and Vitoraz.

After the war, the postal authorities had to take energetic measures to avert the threatened disorganization of the postal service, because of the sudden interruption of the old organization of the postal service, the lack of material, and the shortage of trained employees. The first problem was to regain for the postal service the confidence of the public which had been largely lost during the war (since

1920 the losses of mails have decreased from 0.44 per cent to 0.08 per cent and are still decreasing). It was necessary to improve the organization and extend the service in all directions. For this purpose transportation of mail by aeroplane was established and the automobile transportation was extended.

In Austria-Hungary, the transportation of mail by aeroplane was almost unknown. In the summer of 1920, the Czechoslovakak Postal Administration concluded an agreement with the French-Rumanian Aerial Transportation Company, and the aerial transportation of mail between Prague, Strasburg and Paris was inaugurated in October, 1920. In January of 1921, the aerial route was extended to Warsaw, and at present a route is in operation also between Vienna and Prague with a connection for Budapest. Later on the service is to be extended to Belgrade and Bucharest. Czechoslovakia is also negotiating with Switzerland in regard to the establishment of an aerial route between Prague, Munich, Zurich and Geneva, with an extension to Lyons and to Spain. Plans for an aerial mail, to be carried by dirigible airships (direct connection between Prague and North America, South Africa, the Indies, Australia, and Japan) are under consideration.

The French-Rumanian Aerial Company also transports passengers and goods.

Before the war Austria had 42 State automobile routes in service, of a total length of 1,586.56 kilometers; twenty lines with a total length of 470.06 kilometers were in the present territory of Czechoslovakia. During the comparativly short time of five years, and notwithstanding the unfavorable- conditions existing after the war, the Czechoslovak Postal Administration inaugurated regular automobile transportation of mails and passengers on 98 lines of a total length of 2,102 kilometers. For transportation 170 autobuses are used, and for the carrying of letters and parcels 23 light automobiles and 48 trucks are employed. The postal automobile service is administered by 53 offices; the average number of passengers carried during six months is 1,253,846; the number of packages and personal effects is 53,445; the number of kilometers traveled daily is 6,825.

It was naturally in the interest of the state as well as in the interest of commerce and industry that an extensive system of dependable telegraph lines should be built in which Prague would assume a leading position due to its geographical situation. Notwithstanding the lack of material and shortage of skilled workmen, the telegraphic communications within the country have been greatly improved. Thus, for instance, there was formerly only one line between Prague and Bruo, while now there are three direct lines. Other industrial and commercial centers like Přerov and Moravská Ostrava are now connected with Prague by direct lines, and Přerov also has direct communication with Bratislava and Žilina.

Besides the building of new lines, steps were taken toward the improvement of the service by the installation of modern appliances, such as the Hughes, Baudet and Siemens apparatus.

For the telegraphic communication with foreign countries, the postal administration has established and maintains service over direct telegraph lines with France, Prague-Paris: with England, Prague-London; with Poland, Prague-Warsaw; Pŕerov-Cracow, Moravská Ostravea-Bilsko, Žilina-Cracow, Košice-Lvov; with Rumania, Prague-Bucharest, Košice-Bucharest, Košice-Cluj, Košice-Oradeamare; with Yugoslavia, Prague-Belgrade, Prague-Zagreb; with Italy, Prague-Trieste; with Hungary, Prague-Budapest, Brno-Budapest, Košice-Miskolcz; with Austria, Prague-Vienna, České Budéjovice-Vienna, Brno-Vienna, Pŕerov-Vienna, Bratislava-Vienna, Moravská Ostrava-Vienna, Znojmo-Vienna, Bŕeclava-Vienna, Plzeň-Vienna, Karlovy Vary-Vienna, Prague-Linz, České Budéjovice-Linz; with Germany, Prague-Berlin, Prague-Dresden, Prague-Leipsig, Prague-Hamburg, Prague-Munich, Karlovy Vary-Berlin, Plzeň-Leipzig, Ústí nad Labem-Dresden, Liberec-Dresden, Brno-Berlin, Prague-Nuremberg, Karlovy Vary-Hof, Podmoklí-Dresden, Liberec-Svitau, Liberec-Goerlitz, Bratislava-Berlin; and with Switzerland, Prague-Zurich.

The postal administration intends to build powerful radio-telegraphic stations in several large cities, so as to maintain communication with foreign countries in the case of damage to the telegraphic lines. The first broadcasting stations were built in Prague (Král. Vinohrady) and in Brno. Both these stations have been in use since January 1, 1922. The most powerful station is to be that of Podébrady, with a wave length of about 4,000 meters (the Košice and Bratislava stations have wave lengths of over 2,000 meters); it will be used for communication with western Europe, while the Košice station is intended for commununciation with eastern Europe. In Karlovy Vary there is being built a radio-telegraphic station with a wave length of about 1,100 meters. On the governmental aviation field in Kbely there is being erected a radiographic station for the purposes of aviation only.

The transmission of telegrams between Czechoslovakia and the United States of America is done over the direct telegraph wires of Prague-Paris (system Baudet) and Prague-London (system Baudet), thence to Brest-Havre, or over the wires of the British or French cable companies (Anglo-American Telegraph Company, Compagnie Française des Cables Télégraphiques, Commercial Cable Company, Eastern Union Direct United States Cable Company). In consequence of these arrangements, cable communication with the United States of America, as compared with the cable service of other States of Central Europe, is a superior one. When the radio-telegraphic service has established connections with the four large transatlantic radio-telegraphic stations (French, German, Polish, and British), the transmission of messages will be further improved. The cable then will not be so heavily overladen and a lower rate for the transmission of deferred cablegrams, lettergrams, press dispatches, etc., may be introduced. With other distant countries Czechoslovakia communicates largely through the cables of the largest world cable company, the Eastern Telegraph Company. Dispatches to South America are directed via France, but later on may also be directed via Italy, for that country is now laying a cable to South America.

During the former régime, there were only a few

direct telephone lines between the important industrial centers of Bohemia and Vienna, and the same may be said about Slovakia and Budapest. There were, however, no direct internal lines connecting Bohemia with Moravia and Slovakia, the establishment of which was one of Czechoslovakia's first tasks.

The telephone service with Austria has been improved as has also the service with Germany. At present Czechoslovakia possesses two direct telephone lines to Berlin, Dresden, Leipzig, and Nuremberg. Děčin also has a direct telephone line to Dresden. With Poland telephone communication has also been established. At present other direct lines are being constructed for communication with Germany: Prague-Berlin, Prague - Hamburg, Karlovy Vary - Chemnitz, and Liberec-Goerlitz. A direct line is planned for the connections Prague-Zurich, Prague-Budapest, and Prague-Zagreb.

Shortly after its establishment, the Czechoslovak Republic became a member of the World Postal Union and a party to the International Telegraph Treaty and the International Radio-telegraph Treaty. Owing to successful negotiations with foreign countries in regard to mutual postal regulations, Czechoslovakia is at present in postal communication with nearly all the countries of the world.

In November, 1921, an international radio-telegraph conference was held at Prague which was attended by representatives of all the succession States of Austria-Hungary, and of Germany and Bulgaria. The conference concluded agreements concerning the establishment of direct international telegraphic lines, rates, the maintenance of lines, the speedy dispatch of telegrams, the settlement of complaints, etc.

The postal organization of Czechoslovakia includes a Postal Checking Bureau, established by the law of March 11, 1919 (No. 140 of the Collection of Laws and Regulations). The Bureau is a State institution under the direct supervision of the Ministry of Posts and Telegraphs. Through the post offices the Bureau accepts deposits for the persons or firms who have established accounts with the Bureau, and checks issued by the holders of the accounts are credited to the payees or paid in cash. The post offices throughout the State act as agents of the Bureau; they accept deposits and pay out money on orders of the Bureau. On December 31, 1921, the Postal Checking Bureau held the following balances in the countries listed:

	No. of depositors	Total deposits (in millions)	No. of transactions	Total turnover in 1921 (in millions)
Czechoslovak (Czechoslovak crowns)	63,739	2,399	49,917,198	162,546
Belgium (francs)......	65,514	715	15,918,409	55,733
Holland (gulden).......	55,410	138	7,634,528	6,967
Japan (yen)	180,683	37	36,300,009	2,382
Hungary (Magyar crowns)	40,475	2,993	7,871,936	147,580
Germany (marks).....	759,830	10,998	428,163,000	1,192,445
Austria (Austrian crowns)	177,465	33,893	39,784,677	981,142
Switzerland (francs)...	42,740	126	25,096,230	17,776

The postal administration employs 18,575 clerks of whom 73.8 per cent are Czechs and Slovaks, 24 per cent Germans and 2.2 per cent of other races. The postal administration also employs 18,941 mail carriers, chauffeurs, etc.

At present there are in Czechoslovakia 4,605 post offices and 3,688 telegraph offices. Automobiles mail is carried by 185 autobuses, 23 light automobiles and 48 trucks. For the transportation of mail by railroads there are over 800 mail cars. The volume of mail carried daily is over 15,000,000 pieces of letter mail (including newspapers and printed matter) and over 280,000 parcels.

The telegraph wires in use measure 126,826 kilometers. Telegrams average 256,577 per week and 1,026,307 per month.

The length of the interurban telephone wires is 77,802 kilometers, the local telephone wires measure 167,416 kilometers. There are 1,348 telephone centrals, and 85,717 subscribers. The number of local calls per month averages about 14,000,000, and the long distance calls number over 650,000 per month.

The Ministry of Posts and Telegraphs shows the following revenue and expenditure since its establishment:

From November 1, 1918, to December 31, 1918, the revenue amounted to 17,689,800 crowns and the expenditure to 15,545,500 crowns. For 1919, the revenue was estimated at 177,937,000 Czechoslovak crowns and the expenditure at 160,284,600 crowns. The actual receipts for 1919 were, however, 201,149,000 crowns and the disbursements 187,764,100 crowns. For 1920 the receipts were estimated at 429,801,500 crowns and the expenditure at 420,859,120 crowns. The actual revenue amounted to 528,716,900 crowns and the expenditure to 413,140,200 crowns. In 1921 the receipts were estimated at 802,765,100 crowns and the actual revenue was 828,607,100 crowns and the expenditure 1,026,310,300 crowns. For 1922 the preliminary estimate of receipts was 962,930,500 crowns, and of the expenditure 871,654,970 crowns. The actual realized revenue amounted to 902,277,474 crowns and the expenditure to 869,494,872 crowns. For 1923 the receipts were estimated at 1,162,054,000 crowns, and the expenditure at 880,358,000 crowns, and for 1924 the receipts at 1,089,313,000 crowns and the expenditure at 853,292,770 crowns.

In the expenditure for 1919 and 1920 the high cost of living bonuses paid to the employees from a fund authorized by the Government were not included. In 1921 the bonuses were included in the budget of the Ministry of Posts and Telegraphs, thus causing a deficit in the budget. In 1922, however, the revenue exceeded the expenditure, although the Ministry continued to pay the bonuses.

The receipts of the postal administration would be much higher were it not for the free transportation of a huge volume of official correspondence. The privilege of free mail is also extended to municipal and parochial offices, to charitable institutions, chambers of commerce, etc. In Austria before the war, correspondence of this kind amounted to one-seventh of all the letters carried through the mails. The postal authorities are contemplating a drastic revision of the franking privilege which naturally will bring about a considerable increase in the revenue of the Ministry of Posts and Telegraphs.

XII

BANKING

Karel Karásek, Director of the Industrial and Agricultural Bank of Bohemia, Prague

The old Austro-Hungarian Empire had two economic centers, Vienna and Budapest, which controlled the economic life of the provinces and which, in consequence, became the seat of the largest and most influential banks. The banks themselves favored this economic centralism which was also supported by the Government's policy of taxation. Just as, after the foundation of the German monarchy, the establishment of the large Berlin banks had led to a concentration of economic activities in Berlin to the detriment of Frankfort, Dresden and Hamburg, so the big banks of Vienna helped to maintain the controlling influence of Vienna in Austrian economic life, although about 80 per cent of the industries were concentrated in Bohemia and Moravia.

Under such circumstances it is not surprising that the first banking institution established in Prague in 1857 should have been a branch of the Vienna Oest. Creditanstaldt für Handel und Gewerbe. It was only in 1863 that the first independent bank was established in Prague, and that was the Bohemian Discount Bank, established by German bankers and industrialists of

Prague. In 1867 followed the establishment of the Agricultural Credit Bank for Bohemia, among the founders of which were some Czech noblemen. The first bank was to serve the German financiers and business men, the second was to assist agriculture and the agricultural industries. After the establishment of these two banks the first Czech bank was founded in 1869—The Živnostenská Banka for Bohemia and Moravia—founded, as its name suggests, to promote the interests of trade and industry.

At the end of 1872 there were in Prague nineteen joint-stock banks with an aggregate capital of 44,000,000 florins (1 florin=2 prewar Austrian crowns or $0.405), but their financial reserves were, in most cases, weak as was proved in May, 1873, when the Vienna crisis broke out, for only four of the Prague banks survived the crisis: the Bohemian Discount Bank, the Agricultural Credit Bank, the Živnostenská Banka, and the Bohemian Union Bank. Of the provincial banks only two remained, one of which, transferred later to Prague, has become one of the greatest Czech banks. It is the Prague Credit Bank.

The crisis of 1873 had brought such enormous losses to financial enterprises and so shaken the confidence of the public that for many years economic life appeared to be almost paralyzed. For twenty-five years not a single new joint-stock bank was established in Prague. The Vienna banks, on the other hand, established several new branches in Bohemia. In 1877 a branch of the Anglo-Austrian Bank was established, in 1890 one of the Vienna Bank-Verein, and in 1896 a branch of the Länderbank. A larger basis for banking was created through the development of industry and commerce promoted by the industrial prosperity in 1905 and 1907. In the period of 1898 to 1914, about twenty new joint-stock banks were founded, while the old banks greatly increased their capital. With a few exceptions the new institutions were mostly banks founded by Czechs seeking to counteract the supremacy of German banking, a supremacy due to economic centralism which had benefited Vienna but hampered and retarded the economic development of Bohemia. Down to the end of the last century, the Czech industries remained far behind the German industries, and the energy of the Czech nation in that period was concentrated mainly in agriculture and trade. The foundation, however, was laid for the industrial and commercial development which has taken place in the last two decades. The conditions then prevailing found an expression in the development of Czech banking and its relations to the German banks. At the end of the last century the Czechs had but one great bank (the Živnostenská Banka), while the Germans had two large banks and branches of four Vienna banks. The supremacy was, therefore, on the side of Vienna, which controlled several of the biggest industrial establishments in the Czech territories. In Slovakia, of course, the controlling interest was in the hands of Budapest; up to the outbreak of the war it was hardly possible to speak of Slovak banking. Of the total bank capital in the Czech territories, only about a fourth was in the hands of Czech banks at the end of the last century. The development of the Czech banks in the last two decades was therefore an attempt to secure to Czech banking its due place, and the attempt was successful.

The war itself contributed to a great extent to the favorable development of Czech banking. The banks in Austria, as a matter of fact, did not suffer through the war; the balance sheets of the banks in Czech territories show that their war losses were insignificant. The inflation and the depreciation of the currency were no doubt the main causes of the comparative prosperity of the banks during the war, for, through the inflation, both industries and banks were enabled to realize considerable profits. Bank deposits increased steadily, and the Czech banks in particular profited by the prosperity of the farmers. The Czech peasant is known as intelligent and industrious, and his savings made during the war were deposited in Czech banks. So it happened that through the war and through the establishment of the Czechoslovak Republic, Czech banking gained considerable advantages over the German banks.

In the Czech territories, with the exception of Slovakia, there are at present thirty-seven joint-stock banks. Of these ten are in German hands and twenty-seven in Czech hands. These banks have about 25 billion crowns of paid-up capital and deposits. Of this total 10 billion may be credited to German banks and 15 billion to Czech banks, so that the ratio between Czech and German banks which had been 25:75 at the end of the last century has been changed to 60:40.

To complete our exposition we now give the balance sheets of fourteen large Czechoslovak banks each with a paid-up capital exceeding 50 million crowns. Four of these fourteen banks are in German hands: the Bohemian Discount Bank, which has taken over the branches of the Oesterr. Credit-Anstalt; the Bohemian Union Bank; the Bank for Commerce and Industry, which was established through the conversion of the branches of the Oesterr. Länderbank into an independent bank; and the Bohemian Commercial Bank, which was founded through the consolidation of the branches of the Vienna "Merkur" bank. The paid-up capital, with reserves, in million crowns, is shown in the following table:

	1900	1905	1910	1914	1918	1920	1921	1922
Zivnostenská Banka	29	36	80	111	169	303	334	349
Bohemian Discount Bank.	23	28	28	29	31	165	228	279
Bohemian Industrial & Agricultural Bank	..	..	..	..	..	..	198	270
Anglo-Czechoslovak Bank.	..	..	..	..	..	..	..	167
Moravian Agrarian & Industrial Bank	..	..	8	15	47	198	192	198
Bank for Commerce & Industry	..	..	..	..	..	..	117	120
Bohemian Commercial Bk.	..	..	..	..	..	58	95	101
Prague Credit Bank.....	7	9	32	41	85	132	130	137
Gen. Czech B'king Union.	..	..	..	..	..	..	..	88
Bank of the Czechoslovak Legions	..	..	..	..	..	..	81	89
Bohemian Agrarian Bank	..	..	..	4	13	86	87	87
Bohemian Bank	..	..	4	8	22	72	74	75
Moravian Discount Bank.	..	..	..	..	..	..	38	51

DEPOSITS IN CURRENT AND SAVINGS ACCOUNTS IN MILLION CROWNS

	1900	1905	1910	1914	1918	1920	1921	1922
Zivnostenská Banka	103	125	248	295	1,567	4,229	4,718	4,316
Bohemian Discount Bank.	49	71	120	155	392	2,080	2,494	2,383
Bohemian Industrial & Agricultural Bank	..	..	..	..	..	..	1,160	2,383
Bohemian Union Bank..	91	122	232	241	754	1,933	2,394	2,383
Anglo-Czechoslovak Bank.	..	..	27	34	418	1,110	1,350	1,122
Bank for Commerce and Industry	..	..	..	..	..	..	959	1,238
Bohemian Commerecial Bk.	..	..	..	..	..	457	857	879
Prague Credit Bank.....	23	32	56	81	340	1,396	1,464	1,410
Gen. Czech B'king Union.	..	..	..	..	..	..	..	827
Bank of the Czechoslovak Legions	..	..	..	..	..	..	293	486
Bohemian Agrarian Bank.	..	..	..	16	469	998	1,204	1,227
Bohemian Bank	..	..	14	22	76	305	451	520
Moravian Bank	..	..	..	..	..	..	223	317

These figures illustrate the development of Czechoslovak banking since the end of the last century. They show how small the capital of the banks was twenty-two years ago, amounting to only about 400 million crowns; they show further how the capital rapidly increased from 1905 to 1910 to 1,055 millions, and finally they show the effects of the monetary inflation during and after the war. The capital of the banks increased in the years 1914 to 1918 from 1,338 million crowns to 5,254 millions, increasing approximately four times, the increase nearly corresponding to the depreciation of the crown at home. The depreciation continued, however, and by the end of 1921 the banking capital had increased to 19,467 million crowns, i. e., about fourteen times in comparison with the year 1914. And such was, in fact, the prewar depreciation of the currency at home, *i.e.,* so many times the cost of living had increased in comparison with prewar times. This is undoubtedly an interesting fact showing the connection between the value of the currency and the nominal amount of banking capital.

Having described the development of Czechoslovak banks we shall now investigate their transactions, their enterprise, and their relation to the economic life of the country. In the rich western European countries industry and commerce were established long before the foundation of a banking system; they were the result of a development extending through centuries which needed no banks in its early stages. The banks have not only assisted the economic development—they served commerce and industry and were, at the same time, reservoirs of capital. In Central Europe, however, the case was, in many instances, quite the reverse. Here the task of the banks was to establish industry and commerce, to help in the foundation of new industrial concerns, to seek the commercial highways of the world, while, at the same time, as in Western Europe, accepting deposits from all parts of the country and from all classes of the population. In this way, in Central Europe, in Germany, Austria, Hungary and Italy, the type of a universal bank was founded, a bank doing all-around business and serving comparatively well the economic and financial needs of the population.

The Czechoslovak banks, too, are of this general character. The industrial development in the Czechoslovak territories was slow, for there were few capitalists. This explains why in Bohemia the industrial and banking development has had a more democratic character than elsewhere. The Czech banks have grown up from small beginnings, all classes of population participating in their foundation, so that the shares of the Czech banks are in the hands of people of all classes. There are really no Czech banks exclusively controlled by big financial groups. Owing to the slow development of industry in Bohemia there were but few industries with a large capital, and consequently an active participation of the banks in industrial concerns became necessary. This participation took the form of large credits to manufacturers and partly of direct organization of companies which would then take over large private concerns or found new ones. This direct assistance to industry was one of the main activities of the Czechoslovak banks.

The following table shows the investment of the funds of the Czechoslovak banks:

ASSETS IN 1922

(in million crowns)

Banks:	Short-term loans	Bills and notes	Stocks and other securities	Debtors
Živnostenská Banka	369	790.6	110.5	3,176.4
Bohemian Discount Bank..	150.9	140.9	118.3	2,349.5
Bohemian Industrial & Agricultural Bank	161.5	356.7	154.6	1,870.3
Bohemian Union Bank.....	214.8	216.3	148.7	2,075.7
Anglo-Czechoslovak Bank..	117.5	120.3	155.1	1,080
Moravian Agrarian and Industrial Bank	25.4	38.8	117.9	1,137.1
Bank of Commerce & Industry	111.5	99.5	47.4	1,119.1
Bohemian Commercial Bank	73.7	38	25	886.8
Prague Credit Bank.......	35.3	297.8	104.6	1,050.8
General Czech Banking Union	136.1	19.7	23.4	743.8
Bank of Czechoslovak Legions	85.1	22.5	34.9	363.6
Bohemian Agrarian Bank...	100.9	25.7	271.2	849.5
Bohemian Bank	45.7	41.9	71.9	419.5
Moravian Discount Bank...	65.6	46	8.8	249.7

The reserve for current payments includes cash on hand and demand obligations, totaling in excess of 2 billion crowns, and a reserve of negotiable paper which may be rediscounted at the banking office of the Ministry of Finance. These represent about 25 per cent of the deposits and may be considered a sufficient reserve. In this connection it should be mentioned that bills of exchange are now fewer than formely, as payments in cash are now more in favor. The banks hold about a billion crowns, partly in Government bonds and partly in industrial bonds, the latter showing the influence of the banks in industrial concerns. The banks hold from 10 to 30 per cent of the capital stock of various companies which, together with the credits granted, is sufficient for their control. The greatest asset is represented, however, by the debtors holding credits granted to industrial concerns. These credits are often secured by real estate mortgages, bonds, etc. Through these activities the banks control the economic life of the country because they alone are able to grant the credits necessary to industrial enterprises.

Besides the general banking business, the Czechoslovak banks deal also in bonds and other securities, buy and sell foreign exchange, and arrange for payment abroad. All the great banks have connections with foreign banks, especially with the banks in Germany, Yugoslavia, France, Italy, England, and the United States.

To show the activities of the Czechoslovak banks it is necessary to show their profits and expenses. These are shown in the table on the following page.

Most of the profits are derived from interest, *i.e.*, from the difference between the interest on deposits and loans. The banks pay at present 4 to 4½ per cent interest on deposits, but demand 7 and 7½ per cent. Moreover, they receive a commission on checking accounts, on foreign exchange and similar transactions. Profits made on deals in securities, bonds, etc., are included under the heading of "various profits." Expenses are large so that the net profits of the banks are not extensive. Dividends paid by the banks amount to about 6 to 14 per cent of the paid-up capital. Before the war the highest dividend was about 8 per cent. As nearly all banks pay good dividends the shares of the banks are in great demand by investors.

The banks, as a rule, do not show all their profits,

for they are anxious to build up internal reserves for unforeseen losses, and thus to strengthen the confidence of the public.

On the whole, Czechoslovak banking is in a very satisfactory state. The Czechoslovak banks have developed into strong financial institutions fully satisfying the economic needs of an independent State and promising well for the future. As the Czechoslovak Republic is likely to become a creditor of the weaker eastern European countries, the Czchoslovak banks can not but gain in their importance and activities.

PROFITS AND LOSSES IN 1922

(in million crowns)

Banks:	Interest Paid	Interest Received	Commission	Various profits	Administrative expenses	Taxes	Other expenses	Net profits
Zivnostenská banka	216.4	313.7	45	13	77.7	22.1	5.3	52.2
Bohemian Discount Bank	58	139.2	27.6	21.3	68.5	25	5	32
Bohemian Industrial & Agricultural Bk.	90.2	153.7	28	13.6	60.6	11.2	4	32.3
Bohemian Union Bk.	74.5	148.2	41.4	26	82.4	22.4	3.9	33.1
Anglo-Czechoslovak Bank	53.1	87	26.5	1.3	43	7.3	0.7	20.2
Moravian Agric. & Indus. Bank	106.2	130.1	21.7	2.5	20.8	2.9	8.3	16.1
Bank for Commerce and Industry	64.3	93.4	15.2	3.3	22.1	10	0.1	16.2
Bohemian Commercial Bank	22.9	45.5	11.4	14.1	27.4	2.7	4.4	13.7
Prague Credit Bank	78.8	116.6	17.2	12	34.9	7.8	2.9	21.7
Gen. Czech Banking Union	44.5	66	15.4	7.8	26.3	7.5	2.1	8.9
Bank of Czechoslovak Legions	22	37.1	8.7	2.8	14.4	0.6	6.3	5.4
Bohemian Agrarian Bank	55.9	74.7	11.8	5.5	17.9	4.3	9.6	6.5
Bohemian Bank	9.4	19.1	7.8	2.6	9.5	2.5	1.3	6.9
Moravian Discount Bank	14	24.1	4.1	2	6.8	3.3	1.3	5.1

XIII

CURRENCY CONDITIONS

DR. VILIBALD MILDSCHUH, PROFESSOR AT THE CHARLES UNIVERSITY, PRAGUE

1. THE SITUATION AT THE TIME OF THE ESTABLISHMENT OF THE REPUBLIC

The limited financial resources of the former Empire compelled the Government of Austria-Hungary to cover its war expenditure by the issue of bank notes. On July 23, 1914, the total circulation of bank notes in Austria-Hungary had been only 2,129 million crowns; during the war it increased by October 26, 1918, to 30,679 million crowns, an increase of 28,550 million crowns. As the total national income of Austria-Hungary was estimated before the war at 19 billion crowns, it will be seen that the increase of currency during the war amounted to 150 per cent of the total national income and that the money income had therefore increased to the same extent, although there was no increase in the economic values. As a natural result, the cost of living increased with the income. Exact figures relating to the increase of prices in Austria-Hungary during the war are not available, but it may be safely estimated that at the end of the war the prices were about five times the prewar prices, although, on account of Government control. the prices of some agricultural products and the rents were kept at the old level.

With the decline in the buying power of the Austrian crown its exchange value also declined. At first the decline was not very marked, for, on October 25, 1918, the Austrian crown was still valued in Zurich at about 44 Swiss centimes. When, however, the old monarchy collapsed and new States arose out of its ruins, with Czeschoslovakia the first among them, the exchange value of the Austro-Hungarian crown declined rapidly, and there were reasons to expect that the decline would continue. That would naturally depress the value of the Austrian war loan bonds. Consequently, the holders of the war bonds endeavored to turn the war loan bonds into cash, as the Austro-Hungarian Bank was bound to make advances on them up to 75 per cent of their nominal value. There was, therefore, an imminent danger that the war bonds would soon be turned into bank notes and the evils of monetary inflation increased. There was another dangerous possibility, namely, that the Austro-Hungarian Bank would issue new bank notes for the credit of the various succession States and thus bring about a depreciation of the currency even in those States which did not issue any new notes. Dr. Rašín, the first Czechoslovak Minister of Finance, hoped at first to check this danger by negotiations with the Austro-Hungarian Bank. When, however, these negotiations failed to bring the desired results (the Austro-Hungarian Bank continued to make advances on the war loan bonds and to print new bank notes), Dr. Rašín decided to take independent measures. He prohibited the branches of the Austro-Hungarian

Bank in Czechoslovak territory to make any further advances on the war bonds; established an independent Czechoslovak postal savings department; refused to recognize the new provisional Austrian twenty-five, two hundred, and ten thousand crown notes; and made preparations for a complete separation of the Czechoslovak from the Austro-Hungarian currency by stamping the notes circulating in the Czechoslovak territory.

The stamping of the notes was done in the week of March 3-9, 1919, under the authority of a law passed by the National Assembly on February 25th. In the night of that same day, February 25th, all frontier traffic was stopped until March 9th, to prevent the importation of new bank notes. Only notes of ten, twenty, fifty, one hundred, and one thousand crowns were stamped, and the one and two-crown bank notes were provisionally left in circulation unstamped. Later on, however, in the fall of 1919, when the Czechoslovak State notes, printed in America, were ready, these one and two-crown bank notes, together with the stamped bank notes, were withdrawn from circulation and exchanged for Czechoslovak State notes. In this way the separation of the Czechoslovak currency was carried out relatively early and easily. The necessity and timeliness of this action was soon demonstrated by the differences in the movement of the Austrian and the Czechoslovak exchange.

At the time of the stamping of the bank notes, Dr. Rašín retained one-half of the bank notes submitted for stamping as an enforced State loan. Some of the amounts thus retained were, however, released later, so that the sum retained did not exceed 28.69 per cent of the total amount of 7,436 million crowns of stamped notes. For the retained amounts the owners received 1 per cent State certificates which were to be paid in the coming years out of the revenue derived from the levy on capital and from the tax on the increase of capital during the war, and these measures were introduced at the same time. Until then the bank notes thus retained were to be kept in the banking department of the Ministry of Finance and not to be placed in circulation. Through these measures Dr. Rašín sought to reduce the amount of the fiduciary circulation in order to place the finances of the State on the regular credit system, so that everything the State needed could be obtained through regular credits granted by the bank of issue, or, as was the case in Czechoslovakia, by the Banking Department of the Ministry of Finance acting provisionally as a bank of issue. As a matter of fact there was at that time such an abundance of paper currency that the banks paid only one per cent interest on deposits, and the object of Dr. Rašín, the reduction of the fiduciary circulation, was fully accomplished by those measures.

II. The Movement of Prices

By the separation of its currency Czechoslovakia put a stop to monetary inflation, yet in the years 1919 and 1920 prices in Czechoslovakia increased considerably, though not to such an extent as in the neighboring countries. There was an increase of prices not only in the first year after the war, when prices everywhere showed an upward tendency, but also in the second year after the war, when in England and elsewhere the prices showed a downward tendency.

The enormous increase of prices in Czechoslovakia in 1920 is strikingly shown in a comparison of the prewar index of prices with that of 1920. At the time of writing no official figures as to the increase of prices are available, but reliable data relating to the increase of prices of the principal products have been compiled. Taking 100 as an equivalent of the prices current in the first half of 1914, the prices of the principal articles at the end of 1920 were as follows: Flour 460 (price fixed by the Government), beer 857, sugar 964, firewood 1,142, beef 1,190, cowhides 1,675, petroleum 1,786, butter 1,929, coal 2,134, iron 2,682, cotton cloth 4,268. The average of the prices was 1,542, so that the prices in Czechoslovakia had increased 15.5 times over the prewar level, an increase which, in comparison with western European countries, was unusually large. In this connection it is necessary to mention that the prices of some commodities, such as flour, sugar, and rent, were controlled by the Government; otherwise the prices of these articles would have been much higher.

In 1921 and 1922 the movement of wholesale prices was as follows (official figures; July, 1914, prices taken at 100):

	Jan.	Feb.	March	April	May	June
1921............	1,458	1,460	1,317	1,323	1,326	1,270
1922............	1,675	1,520	1,552	1,491	1,471	1,471
	July	Aug.	Sept.	Oct.	Nov.	Dec.
1921............	1,259	1,361	1,653	1,654	1,681	1,674
1922............	1,464	1,386	1,155	1,059	1,017	999

It will be observed that the prices reached the highest point at the end of 1920 and began to decline in the beginning of 1921, and that by July of that year the prices had decreased nearly 20 per cent. But in the second half of 1921 a new increase of prices is to be observed. This increase was, of course, the result of the abolition of the Government control of prices of the principal agricultural products and of the re-establishment of the freedom of the internal trade. The former alone does not explain the great increase of prices, for the withdrawal of Government control accounted for 244 points only, while the actual increase between July and December, 1921, was 415 points. In 1922 there was, however, a steady decline of prices which was especially rapid in August of that year.

III. Internal Financial Conditions

What was the cause of the downward movement of prices in Czechoslovakia coming so late? Was it monetary inflation?

Here we may draw attention to the fact that the unfortunate consequences to which the monetary inflation had led in former Austria-Hungary and in the neighboring countries were one of the main reasons for the Czechoslovak Government to take measures to stop further monetary inflation. This was accomplished by the law of April 10, 1919, which provides in section 10 that the total circulation of uncovered notes must be limited to the amount of the notes originally stamped, plus the amount of notes used up to one-half of the total amount of the checking accounts and scrip taken over by the Czechoslovak Republic from the Austro-Hungarian Bank, and the amount of the one and two-crown notes circulating in the Czechoslovak territory. Any further increase of circulation is permitted only if the notes are fully covered by gold and silver, or by discounted bills, advances on stocks and shares, and foreign bills. By this law the monetary inflation, it is true, was not completely prevented, for even then the State could again obtain advances in notes at the Banking Office of the Ministry of Finance, but the possibility of inflation was, nevertheless, reduced to narrow limits by the passage of this law. As a matter of fact, there has never been any monetary inflation in Czechoslovakia. This is proved by the returns of the Czechoslovak Banking Office. According to these returns, the monetary situation in Czechoslovakia developed as follows:

	(In thousand Czechoslovak crowns) September 15			
	1920	1921	1922	1923
Notes in circulation	9,891,346	11,253,828	9,837,009	8,925,099
Discounts	906,273	857,157	321,485	585,416
Advances on securities	2,249,956	2,516,424	1,559,055	925,351
Foreign bills and balances	303,949	803,849	1,736,393	2,444,593
Gold and silver holdings	252,808	593,128	727,665	1,060,763
Unsecured circulation	6,178,360	6,483,270	5,492,411	3,908,976
Legal maximum circulation of notes	10,452,454	11,787,438	11,343,835	12,020,145
Note reserve	561,108	533,610	1,506,826	3,095,046

The increase or decrease in the circulation of notes does not depend on the needs of the State, but is affected mainly by commerciel needs.

IV. External Causes Affecting the Prices

It is therefore necessary to inquire whether the causes of the increase or decrease of Czechoslovak prices may be found in external influences, especially in the rate of exchange of the Czechoslovak currency. In the fluctuation of foreign exchange both the increase and the decrease in the rate usually correspond to a contrary movement of prices. In the case of Czechoslovakia the increase of prices until the end of 1921, and the following decrease, correspond first to the decrease and then to the increase in the rate of exchange of the Czechoslovak crown.

What were the causes affecting the changes in the rate of exchange of the Czechoslovak crown? Here we may consider, first of all, the fluctuations in the supply of and the demand for the Czechoslovak crowns both of which have their origin in the changes in the trade balance. Was the trade balance of Czechoslovakia in the years 1919-1921 so unfavorable and the demand for foreign currencies so great as to affect the rate of exchange to such an extent, or has Czechoslovak trade balance in 1922 improved so much as to cause such a great demand for Czechoslovak currency? Nothing of the kind has happened. In 1919 Czechoslovakia had no official statistics of imports and exports, but on the basis of the import and export licenses granted it has been calculated that the imports exceeded the exports by 1,231 million Czechoslovak crowns. The excess of imports was therefore not very great. For 1920 and 1921 official statistics of the Czechoslovak foreign trade have been published, showing that in 1920 the exports exceeded the imports by 4,185 million Czechoslovak crowns and in 1921 by 4,878 million Czechoslovak crowns. In 1922 the foreign trade balance was in favor of Czechoslovakia to the amount of 5,391 million Czechoslovak crowns. It is evident that the great decline of the Czechoslovak crown in the years 1919-1921 could not have been caused by an unfavorable balance of trade.

It appears, therefore, that the causes of the decline of the Czechoslovak crown until the end of 1921, and of the following rise of the Czechoslovak crown, can not be sought in the fluctuations of supply and demand, nor in any other obvious facts, but rather in the changes of the point of view regarding the Czechoslovak crown. What were the influences affecting that change of foreign opinion? The development of the German mark is, in this respect, highly instructive. Until the end of 1921 we see a surprising similarity in the development of the mark and of the Czechoslovak crown. Just as the Czechoslovak crown declined between May, 1919, and February, 1920, from 25 to 5 Swiss centimes, so also the German mark dropped from 41 centimes on June 28, 1919, to 5.62 on January 26, 1920. An improvement in the crown rate was accompanied by a rise in the rate of exchange of the German mark to 18.60 centimes on May 20, 1920, which again was followed in both cases by a decrease. The mark stood at 7.70 centimes in the middle of November, 1920. Another small rise to 10.55 occurred in February, 1921, followed however by a new and steady decline which was much greater in the case of the German mark than in the case of the Czechoslovak crown, so that in August, 1921, the exchange rate of the mark in Zurich was much lower than that of the Czechoslovak crown. The difference between the Czechoslovak crown and the mark increased steadily, especially so after November, 1921, when the Czechoslovak crown began to rise while the mark continued to fall. The similarity in the course of the German mark and the Czechoslovak crown until the fall of 1921 would become still more obvious if it were shown on a diagram.

This similarity shows that in both cases, in the development of the mark as well as in the development of the Czechoslovak crown, the same causes were operating. The cause affecting the German mark, as is generally known, was the expectation that on account of the reparation payments German currency would steadily depreciate. There was also another contributing factor, namely, the expected monetary inflation on the part of Germany. Czechoslovakia, on the other hand, as a victorious State, was not burdened with reparations and the country was practically free from monetary inflation. But owing to insufficient knowledge of the economic resources of Czechoslovakia and to its close economic relations with Germany, the Czechoslovak crown was placed abroad on a level with the German mark. When, however, in the fall of 1921, the mark began to decline rapidly it had become evident that there was no reason to class the Czechoslovak crown with the mark, and consequently the Czechoslovak crown was valued differently, and its rate of exchange started on an independent course. The circumstances which had existed before, namely, the rich economic resources, the absence of monetary inflation, a favorable trade balance, etc., were now fully appreciated as justifying the belief that in the future the crown would improve rather than depreciate.

The consequence of this just expectation was that the Czechoslovak crown which, as we have seen, had for a long time been quoted below its purchasing power at home, and was therefore undervalued, now, after its rapid rise in July, 1922, was quoted abroad above its internal buying power, and consequently was overvalued in comparison with other currencies. How far the Czechoslovak crown was undervalued or overvalued can be approximately ascertained by a comparison of the levels of prices existing in Czechoslovakia and abroad at certain periods (October 1920, May 1921, January 1922 and September 1922). The value of the monetary units of the foreign countries, when expressed in Czechoslovak crowns, ought to correspond to the ratio of prices if the Czechoslovak crown were neither overvalued nor undervalued. If then the actual exchange value of the foreign monetary unit, as expressed in Czechoslovak crowns, is higher than the value calculated on the basis of prices, then the Czechoslovak crown is undervalued in comparison with the foreign unit; if, however, the value of the foreign unit, as expressed in Czechoslovak crowns, is lower, then the Czechoslovak crown is overvalued.

The following table shows how the Czechoslovak crown, compared with the monetary units of other countries in accord with this calculation, was either overvalued (+) or undervalued (—):

(Per mille)

	Oct. 16, 1920	May 16, 1921	Jan. 16, 1922	Sept. 12, 1922
England	—123	—68	—13	+ 34
United States	—114	—42	— 1	+ 46
Italy	— 60	—72	— 9	+ 61
Germany	— 4	— 7	+63	+145

From this table we can clearly see how greatly the

Czechoslovak crown was undervalued in the second half of 1920 as compared with the monetary units of the western states. In the second half of 1922 this undervaluation of the Czechoslovak crown was turned into a considerable overvaluation. In 1923, however, due to the decline of prices in Czechoslovakia, the rate of exchange of the Czechoslovak crown corresponded fairly well with its buying power at home.

V. The Consequences of Undervaluation and Overvaluation of the Currency.

Every considerable and lasting undervaluation or overvaluation of the currency must of necesssity have important consequences for the whole economic life of a country, and such has also been the case with Czechoslovakia. When the currency of a country is undervalued, as was the case in Czechoslovakia from the second half of 1919 with slight variations until the end of 1921, it is possible to receive for the exported goods, even if the prices abroad do not rise, more units of the domestic currency. As the wages, the prices of raw materials, and other expenses at home do not change in the beginning at least, the exporters obtain a special gain the consequence of which is an increase of production, full employment, improvement of the trade balance, and also an improvement in the rate of exchange, if not counterbalanced by other stronger forces. With the increased demand of the manufacturers for raw materials and workmen, the prices of the raw materials and the wages of the workmen increase also and the increased income stimulates the demand at home for other goods, and there are better prospects for other branches of production. These effects are on the whole similar to those produced by monetary inflation. The other side of this state of affairs is, however, that with a depreciated currency the prices of imported goods also increase, and later on the prices of the export goods, too; there is an increase in the cost of living, wages, salaries, and taxes must, of necessity, be increased, and the cost of production rises again and the index of prices goes steadily up. In order to check the increase of the prices, the Government subsidizes the imports of necessaries, assumes control of production, and eventually also monopolizes the sale of goods.

All these consequences were to be observed in Czechoslovakia. The Czechoslovak exports increased (in 1920 the exports were 69,022,209 quintals, but rose to 97,427,354 quintals in 1921, and to 94,902,625 quintals in 1922) and the trade balance was more and more favorable. The profits of the exporters were proportionally high, and the Government sought to obtain a share of them by high export duties, or by control of the exportation of some of the more profitable articles such as sugar, alcohol, malt, etc. The income of the Czechoslovak State from these sources in the years 1919, 1920, and 1921, amounted in the case of sugar to over 5 billion Czechoslovak crowns, and in the case of alcohol and malt to over 1 billion crowns. Unemployment, in comparison with the western states, was proportionately small. Thus, for instance, according to the figures of the Czechoslovak State Statistical Office, the number of the registered unemployed in the beginning of 1921 amounted to 100,000 and varied between 60,000 and 100,000 for a time. The number of the unemployed amounted to about 3 per cent of the total number of workmen. On the other hand, in the second half of 1919 and in the years 1920 and 1921 the prices went steadily upward, the population depending on salaries and fixed incomes suffered, while the unearned profits of the owners of supplies and of the producers and manufacturers increased. In consequence of the increase of the cost of living, the State subsidized the imports of cereals and flour, which again resulted in an increase of taxes and the consequent further rise in the cost of living. At the end of 1921 the causes referred to above brought about a complete change at last, the undervaluation disappeared and was followed shortly afterward, in July, 1922, by an overvaluation of the Czechoslovak crown.

What are the consequences of an overvaluation of currency? First of all, the exports diminish, for even if the prices abroad remain the same, the profits as expressed in the home currency decrease considerably even though the labor expenses at home remain the same. The consequence is that the exportation of certain goods becomes impossible and the production therefore diminishes, the trade balance becomes less favorable, and that again tends to depress the rate of exchange. With these consequences unemployment goes hand in hand, there is less demand for workmen and raw materials, wages go down and prices of raw materials decline, the demand for domestic goods also decreases, and the industrial crisis sets in. However, with the improvement in the rate of exchange the imported as well as the exported goods become cheaper, there is a corresponding decrease in the cost of living; salaries, wages, and taxes can be reduced, and the result is the reduction in the cost of production and consequently also in the price of manfactured goods. With the decline of prices, the rate of exchange rises, etc.

These consequences also may be observed in Czechoslovakia at the time of the increase in the rate of exchange of the Czechoslovak crown. The trade balance became less favorable, unemployment increased, wages were reduced, the prices showed a downward tendency. It is interesting to note that when the prices had gone down so far as to correspond with the rise in the rate of exchange, the exchange showed again an upward tendency.

VI. Conclusions.

The foreign quotations of the Czechoslovak currency fluctuated, as we have seen, from one extreme to another, from a considerable undervaluation to a considerable overvaluation. Both of these phenomena produce unfavorable results. The currency conditions are sound only when the currency is neither undervalued nor overvalued and is stabilized. But how is stabilization to be achieved?

It is often assumed that it is sufficient to introduce the gold standard, for in that case the circumstances that would otherwise lead to an increased rate of exchange (favorable balance of trade, etc.), will result in an influx of gold and the exchange will remain steady, while in the opposite case the factors that would otherwise cause a decline of the exchange, will be counterbalanced by exports of gold. However, for the introduction, and especially for the maintenance of the gold standard, certain things are indispensable. It is necessary, first of all, to establish an economic and financial balance. In this respect Czechoslovakia, as we have seen, has sought to avoid all monetary inflation and has endeavored to balance its income and expenditure, and thus to avoid also an inflation in the form of credits. The second condition is an economic and financial balance in those countries with which it is necessary to trade. This, of course, does not depend on one country alone, it can be brought about only by international cooperation. Only when these conditions have been fulfilled will it be possible to bring about a complete stabilization of the currency.

GOVERNMENT FINANCE

Dr. Karel Engliš, Professor at Masaryk's University in Brno, Member of Parliament and former Minister of Finance

Immediately after the establishment of the Czechoslovak Republic the Czechoslovak State finances were naturally in a difficult position. The newly established State was confronted by great tasks such as the creation of an army and an administration, the reconstruction of railroads, and the building of new schools; it had to deal with social problems such as the care of the invalids, unemployment, food subsidies, and all this had to be accomplished in a country exhausted by the war. It was only natural that the performance of these great tasks seriously affected the finances of the State. The resulting crisis was complicated by the collapse of the financial administration throughout the State, and especially in Slovakia, and became all the more acute because ever since its establishment the State had refused to cover the deficits in its finances by the comfortable method of issuing new notes as was unfortunately the case in the neighboring States. Czechoslovakia, on the contrary, decided to cover its deficits by regular credits only. But the obtaining of credits at home was a matter of considerable difficulty on account of the general shortage of money. When, immediately after the establishment of the Republic, the first loan, the so-called National Liberty Loan, was issued, there was, of course, an abundance of paper money, a result of the Austrian currency inflation, and in the course of a few days one billion crowns was subscribed, but when, in the spring of 1919, the Czechoslovak currency had become independent by the stamping of the old Austrian notes circulating in the territory of the new Republic (on which occasion one-half of the privately held notes had been withdrawn from circulation and exchanged for 1 per cent certificates) there soon developed a considerable shortage of money which no doubt was favorable to the exchange value of the crown, but not to the State finances.

The following two internal loans issued in 1919 and in the beginning of 1920 brought in about one-half of the yield of the first National Liberty Loan, so that the financial situation in the spring of 1920 became precarious. The flour subsidy, amounting to billions, was covered by profits made by the State treasury on the exports of sugar, but for the covering of other large deficits no credits whatever could be found, so that there was a great danger that the Government might not be able to avoid an inflation of the currency. The existing difficulties were increased by the decline of the Czechoslovak crown in the winter of 1919 and 1920. At the time of the establishment of the Czechoslovak Republic the Austrian crown then still in circulation in Czechoslovak territory was valued at 25 Swiss centimes. After the Czechoslovak currency became independent in the spring of 1919, the Czechoslovak crown rose to 34 Swiss centimes and then gradually declined to 4 centimes, a decline which was immediately followed by a rapid increase of prices, wages, salaries, and incomes in general. The general increase of prices made necessary an increase in the salaries of the State employees and Government expenditures grew apace.

It became clear to every one that the decline of the crown must be checked as otherwise it would be impossible to prevent new currency inflation and the subsequent collapse of the State finances, as was the case in the neighboring countries. To put a stop to the decline of the crown it was necessary to obtain large internal credits for a time at least until the State finances could be balanced. This task was accomplished within a year.

In the summer of 1920 the Czechoslovak crown began to rise, and in August, 1920, its value rose to 13 Swiss centimes. For a time the Czechoslovak crown became stabilized at about 10 Swiss centimes and continued to be quoted at that rate until the fall of 1921 when an order for the mobilization of the army was issued, owing to the Magyar attempt at the restoration of the Habsburgs. The Czech crown fell to 6 Swiss centimes. It recovered from this decline in the spring of 1922, and in the summer of that year almost trebled its value, rising to about 19 Swiss centimes. The general increase of prices and incomes was stopped, and the finances of the State became normalized.

The second great task consisted in obtaining sufficiently large credits to give the Government time to put the finances of the State in order. We have already explained the difficulties in obtaining credits.

In order to minimize these difficulties the Government consented to accept war loan bonds held by Czechoslovak citizens and institutions in part payment of subscriptions to the new internal loan. It should be mentioned here that, under the peace treaties, Czechoslovakia was not bound to honor the Austrian war loan bonds, but in order to prevent the collapse of some financial institutions, corporations, and individuals, the Government had decided to honor the bonds up to 75 per cent of their nominal value, but only if the bonds were offered as part of a subscription to the new internal loan. Consequently, all those who had war loan bonds of a nominal value of 100 crowns and lent to the State 75 crowns received two State bonds of a nominal value of 75 Czechoslovak crowns each, one replacing the war loan bond and the other representing the cash subscription. Up to the time of writing the new loan has brought in approximately 500 million Czechoslovak crowns and has greatly helped the State to carry on until its finances could be put in order.

The budget for the financial year 1921 amounting to approximately 18 billion Czechoslovak crowns of revenues and 18 billion crowns of expenditure was already balanced. This was accomplished by extensive savings and, above all, by the passage of a financial law which limited the disbursements of the various ministries and made all expenditure in excess of the budget estimates conditional on the consent of the Parliament. On the other hand, the postal fees and railroad rates were readjusted so as to make the railroads paying establishments. There was also some increase in taxes, especially in the tax on luxuries and coal. The estimates of expenditure in the budget for 1921 were not exceeded, although the Government employees received bonuses which were not provided for in the budget.

But the task of the financial administration was not ended, for not only the finances of the State but also the finances of the autonomous communes and the provinces were in difficulties. Here also the crisis was relieved partly by a law providing for a control of communal finances in order to bring about the desired economies, and partly by a 2 per cent increase in the sales tax, which was allocated to the communes. These measures did not, of course, remove all the difficulties, but progress was made in that direction.

In the Budget for 1922, the revenue amounted to 18,884 million and the expenditure to 19,872 million crowns, leaving a deficit of 988 million crowns. The deficit was caused mainly by the inclusion of the uncovered deficits of the provincial administrations in the State expenditure. The State finances suffered somewhat in consequence of the rapid rise of the Czechoslovak crown in the second half of 1922 which will be considered later on.

In 1921 the flour subsidy was abolished, for at that time the profits made on the exports of sugar had nearly disappeared on account of the general decline of the price of sugar in the world markets, and there were no internal financial means to continue the subsidy. Gradually all the remaining central offices for the distribution of food were liquidated and freedom of internal trade was reestablished.

In the budget for 1923 the revenue was estimated at 18,812 million, the expenditure at 19,377 million, leaving a deficit of 565 million crowns. The expenditures of the public administration were covered by the ordinary revenues to the proportion of 96 per cent.

The budget estimates for 1924 are as follows:

	(In Czechoslovak crowns) Expenditure	Revenue
President of the Republic.....	3,000,000	......
Chancellery of the President..	13,674,618	1,790,542
National Assembly	39,361,443	204,000
Supreme Assembly	4,599,619	24,000
Supreme Bd. Financial Control	3,934,425	......
Contributions to communal and provincial administrations...	798,257,000	......
Public debt	1,986,131,074	......
Assistance to orphans, widows, etc., pensions	610,050,360	87,509,000
Ministerial Council	157,496,892	153,102,750
Ministry of Foreign Affairs ...	173,234,118	30,030,000
Ministry of National Defence..	2,299,973,630	172,519,500
Ministry of the Interior.......	599,750,432	7,201,260
Ministry of Education	845,921,810	14,193,878
Ministry of Finance	1,641,080,782	9,077,840,040
Ministry of Commerce	38,712,753	48,989,100
Ministry of Posts and Telegraphs	853,292,770	1,089,313,000
Ministry of Railways	4,174,517,870	4,603,237,530
Ministry of Agriculture	655,366,342	526,476,371
Ministry of Justice	279,881,952	21,214,733
Ministry of Public Works	739,024,793	492,541,267
Ministry of Social Welfare....	786,962,927	8,700,300
Ministry of Supplies	18,764,334	240,000
Ministry of Public Health.....	159,142,893	56,166,230
Ministry of Unification	1,844,068	......
Commission on Repatriation..	110,000,000	......
Total	16,993,976,905	16,391,293,591

It will be observed that in the budget estimates for 1924 the expenditure has been reduced to 16,944 million crowns. This is a reduction of 2,383 million as compared with the preceding year. The special investment budget for the construction of productive public works, such as electric power stations, etc., has been reduced 770 million. The total savings as compared with the preceding year amount to 4,647 millions. The State revenues have decreased to 16,391 millions, the resulting deficit being 603 million, or 44 million greater than in the previous year. The difficulties in the management of the State finances have been caused by the reduction in the coal tax, but the Ministry expects that a reduction in the costs of production will bring about a boom in industry and trade. The expected reductions in the estimated revenue will be made up by a corresponding adjustment of taxation for 1924.

In the second half of 1922 the Czechoslovak crown rose to 19 Swiss centimes, declining later to about 16.75 Swiss centimes, a rate at which it has now been practically stablized ever since January, 1923. The currencies of the neighboring States, especially that of Germany, have, on the other hand, sustained a continual decline, so that the mark has been practically abandoned as a means of savings, while the Czechoslovak crown has been sought as a means of savings on account of its rather increasing value. As a result of the rapid rise of the Czechoslovak crown an industrial crisis and unemployment set in. In view of this fact the writer does not favor monetary deflation, because it has unfortunate consequences for industrial activity and prosperity. Stabilization of the currency is, in the opinion of the writer, the best financial policy to be pursued.

The public debt of Czechoslovakia contracted in Czechoslovak crowns is estimated at approximately 22 billion. The debt includes nearly 7 billion Czechoslovak crowns of liabilities incurred in regulating the currency and in taking over the checking accounts of the Austro-Hungarian Bank, and are as follows:

1. Checking accounts of the Austro-Hungarian bank	6,526,855,144.31
2. State Bank note loan	390,579,000.00
3. Scrip taken over from the Austro-Hungarian Bank	6,971,302,114.31

The internal debts of Czechoslovakia are as follows:

National Liberty Loan, 4 per cent	500,000,000
4 per cent Treasury Notes	1,048,054,000
4½ per cent Premium Loan	540,866,400
5 per cent Treasury Notes	915,990,000
Treasury Bonds (issued in exchange for 6 per cent Treasury Notes)	1,536,185,000
6 per cent Treasury Notes (to cover war expenditure in Slovakia)	677,300,000
Building Lottery Loan, 2 per cent	60,175,947
Public Services Investment Loan (railways, posts and telephones)	589,000,000
Fourth State Loan, 3½ to 6 per cent	3,401,707,736
Currency Loan (to purchase bullion as cover for notes), 3½ per cent	250,000,000
Supplementary credit (for purchase of military equipment), 5 per cent	322,000,000
Flour Loan, 6 per cent	3,400,000,000
Investment Loan for electrification, 6 per cent	10,000,000
6 per cent Treasury Notes	1,830,995,500
	15,082,274,583

The external indebtedness of Czechoslovakia, taking the Czechoslovak crown at 3 cents, is estimated as follows:

1. British Government credits	211,575,472
2. Czechoslovak State Loan	1,033,760,604
3. French Government Credits (for the purchase of military equipment)	229,000,000
for the purchase of horses	36,774,784
for the maintenance of Czechoslovak Army units abroad	77,198,728
4. Italian Government Credit (maintenance of Czechoslovak Army units abroad)	293,400,000
5. United States of America, credits for food, equipment and maintenance of army in Russia	2,917,434,688
6. International (Nansen's) Committee's Credit (for repatriation of prisoners of war in Russia)	12,876,000
7. Revolution Loan (for maintenance of army units abroad)	1,145,000
Total	4,813,165,276

Public debts arising from the Peace Treaties are estimated as follows:

1. Czechoslovak share of Austro-Hungarian pre-war debts, approximately	5,000,000,000
2. Reparation payments under the Treaty of St. Germain, maximum 750,000,000 gold francs, approximately	10,000,000,000
Total	15,000,000,000

In addition, a contingent liability has been incurred by the State through the guaranty of 20 per cent of the international loan to Austria to which Czechoslovakia is a party.

It will be observed, and it is generally admitted, that the Czechoslovak financial policy has been, on the whole, a wise one. The soundness of Czechoslovak State finances proves this beyond doubt, and it is no exaggeration to say that if a like policy had been pursued by other European States the financial reconstruction of Europe would have made a better progress.

XV

LABOR LEGISLATION

Dr. Eugene Štern, Division Chief in the Ministry of Social Welfare

Czechoslovakia has taken over from Austria-Hungary the regulations of the conditions of labor, especially those affecting the labor contract, as they were contained in the civil code. It will be the task of the new State to revise these regulations and to bring them up to date. In the first five years of its existence, Czechoslovakia has enacted a number of laws which have placed the Republic, in the matter of social reform, among the most advanced States.

The Czech nation has always had a tendency toward social reforms. This tendency can be observed in the Hussite movement and in the Church of the Bohemian Brethren as well as in the national renaissance in the beginning of the nineteenth century. In the course of the nineteenth century the Czechoslovak territories were rapidly industrialized; they became the workshop of the former Habsburg Monarchy, but the owners of the industrial plants, mines, iron mills, and landed estates were members of the Austro-German nobility and bourgeoisie, while the workmen were Czechs and Slovaks. Independent Czech industries and commercial houses in which not only the workmen but also the owners were Czechs were established only in the latter part of the last century. The headquarters of the great industrial concerns and of the great banks which had their mines, furnaces, and factories in the present Czechoslovak territories were either in Vienna or in Budapest; and in the social struggles the former Austrian and Hungarian Governments were always hostile to the Czech workmen. Thus in both Austria and Hungary the racial question was at the same time a social question also. The Czech workmen in the Germanized districts of Bohemia had to build their own schools. The connection between the racial and the social question was often emphasized in Professor Masaryk's lectures at the Prague University. He pointed out that the Czech question was above all a social question. Thus it was quite natural that in the newly established State the social question was one of the main preoccupations of the Government and found expression in the steadily expanding social legislation.

Other influences affecting the social legislation are to be found in the repercussions of the Russian social revolution and of the collapse of militarist Germany, as well as in the action of the labor members of the Government. Owing to the advanced standard of popular culture, social legislation in Czechoslovakia has proceeded in a peaceful way without any violent upheavals.

It is impossible to give in this short outline a detailed account of the social legislation; the writer can point out only some of its chief principles.

One of the long-standing demands of the Czech workmen was the eight-hour working day. In 1900 it was the present President of the Czechoslovak Republic, T. G. Masaryk, who emphasized the advantages of the eight-hour working day at a meeting of the miners at Kladno. Before the war the eight-hour working day had been established in some of the key industries and in the mines; after the war it was legally established in most of the European countries. In Czechoslovakia the law establishing the eight-hour day was passed on December 19, 1918.

This law, dictated by the desire to put an end to the war sufferings, marks a new era in Czechoslovakia's social legislation. It includes also regulations of night work and the protection of young workmen and working women. The passage of the law was unanimous, both the representatives of labor and the representatives of industrial capital and agriculture recognizing its necessity.

The main features of the Czechoslovak law providing for an eight-hour working day are the following:

(a) The maximum working day, under the former Austrian laws, was 11 hours in factories, with one hour allowed for overtime. In mines the working day was limited to 9 hours, with 3 hours for eventual overtime. In agriculture and in commercial establishments there was no limitation of working hours whatever.

The new Czechoslovak law limits the working hours to 8 in a day, or 48 in a week, or 192 hours in four weeks, for all categories of labor. The arrangement of the hours is to be determined by agreement between the employers and the employees. In cases of seasonal work, and especially in agriculture and in the building industry, overtime is allowed on application to the boards of labor. Overtime is to be specially paid for in accordance with agreements made between the employers and employees, and must not exceed two hours a day in not more than 20 weeks, or 240 hours in a year.

(b) Pauses in the working hours and Sunday rest.

After five hours of continuous work, the employees are entitled to a rest of at least one-quarter of an hour. It is provided further that once a week the employees must have an uninterrupted rest of at least 32 hours. In establishments in which work can be stopped temporarily, such weekly rest should fall on Sunday; for men engaged in processes requiring continuous operation the weekly rest should be so arranged among the employees as to have every third weekly rest fall on Sunday.

For women employed in factories, the Sunday rest starts on Saturday at 2 o'clock p. m. Exceptions are made only in such cases where the assistance of women is necessary in continuous work. Persons employed in housework are entitled to a weekly rest of at least 18 hours (preferably on Sunday).

(c) Night work. Work at night, that is, from 10 p. m. to 5 a. m., is allowed only in such establishments or public services in which continuous work is necessary. In such work only men over 18 years of age are to be employed. The employment of women in night work is not permitted, but may be allowed in exceptional cases, especially when the work is in the general interest of the public, such as work in the hospitals. In such cases the women employed must be over 18 years of age. House servants must not be given heavy work in the hours from 9 p. m. to 5 a. m., except in emergencies, such as illness in the employer's family, etc.

(d) Protection of children and young persons is partially provided for in the measures regulating night work. It is, however, specially stated in the law that children below 14 years of age must not be employed in enterprises organized for profit, such as factories, etc. In housework and agriculture children over ten years of age may be employed in light work and services only.

The law prohibits the employment of young men up to 16 years of age and young women up to 18 years of age in heavy work which might be detrimental to their health or their physical development. In the mines only men over 16 years may be employed. On the whole, the eight-hour day signifies a stabilization of labor conditions and the end of labor conflicts and strikes for shorter hours, abolition of night work, protection of children, etc.

Protection of Young Workmen

Of great importance is the law of June 17, 1920, regulating the work in the home industries where the employee takes his work home and delivers the finished goods to his employer. This kind of work is known the world over as the sweating system. Attempts to regulate the working hours in the home industries were made in former Austria, but without any practical results. The importance of this question for Czechoslovakia may be judged by the fact that in 1898 there were in the Czech territories alone 226,000 workmen employed in the home industries; including

Slovakia and Carpathian Ruthenia, their number may be estimated at half a million at present.

The law provides for the establishment of district and central committees dealing with the various branches of the home industry. Each committee has nine members who are appointed by the Minister of Social Welfare. One-third of the members are selected from among the employers, another third from among the employees, and the rest from neutral experts. These committees act as mediators in all conflicts between the employers and the employees. The committee usually seeks to effect a compromise, and if this is not possible decides the conflict on its own initiative. The decison is binding on both sides, unless they appeal to the central committee.

The central committees act as appellate bodies and review the decisions of the district committees. They issue rules regulating wages and working conditions of the employees in the home industries. The rules are obligatory on all those employed in the home industries as well as on the employers who have to comply with the conditions prescribed.

The law regulating the working conditions in the home industries is one of the first Czechslovak laws which are not confined to the regulation of working hours and the protection of the workmen's health, but provide also for a minimum wage.

Democratization of Industrial Establishments

After the war the Czechoslovak workmen and their trade unions did not limit their demands to the regulation of the working hours and wages, but demanded also the right to be consulted in regard to the hiring and dismissal of workmen, and a share in the management and profits of the establishment. This demand has had a profound effect on the Czechoslovak social policy. Attempts to satisfy this demand were first made with a partial success in the mining industry.

Under the law of February 25, 1920, district and local miners' councils have been established. The councils are charged with the duty to cooperate in the enforcement of the laws providing for the protection of workmen, to supervise the observance of the wage contracts, to cooperate in the maintenance of discipline in the mines, to act as mediators in conflicts between the employers and employees, and to cooperate in the management of welfare institutions for the employees. The councils are to be consulted in regard to the discharge of workmen. They are authorized to submit plans for improvement of the management, and may examine the annual balance sheets of the concern. The miners' council, however, may not interfere directly with the management of the concern, for its function is mainly advisory.

Local miners' councils are to be elected in all mining establishments employing at least 20 workmen. The council is elected by all employees who are citizens of the Republic, over 18 years of age, and have worked for the concern at least three months in a period of two years. Eligible are those who have worked for the establishment at least six months in three years in the mines, are over 24 years of age, and are citizens of the Republic. The management has one technical and one commercial representative on the council who act as advisers. The meetings of the council take place after the working hours, and the employers may be present.

District councils are elected by the local miners' councils for a period of two years. Their duty is to direct the local councils in the carrying out of the laws regulating the labor conditions, to act as mediators in conflicts between the local miners' councils and the management, to cooperate in the issuing of labor regulations for the entire mining district, in the negotiation of wage contracts, and in the division of the shares of the profits granted by the management to the local council for the benefit of the employees.

The law providing for the establishment of local and district miners' councils has been supplemented by a law providing for a share of the employees in the management and in the profits of the mines. Every mining concern is bound by law to have proper bookkeeping, and to issue an annual balance sheet showing profits or losses. The employees are entitled to a share of 10 per cent of the profits, which is not to be divided among them, however, but to be employed for the general good of the workers. All proceeds received by the local councils go to the district council, which uses them for the support of educational, humanitarian, and other institutions beneficial to the miners.

It was only to be expected that after the establishment of the local and district miners' councils the workmen in other industries would seek to have such councils established also, especially as such councils had already been established in both Austria and Germany. The result of this demand was the passage of the law of August 12, 1921, providing for such factory councils.

These factory councils, however, have nothing in common with those existing in Russia (Soviets), for they are mainly advisory bodies not authorized to interfere in the management of the factories. In accordance with the law a factory council is to be elected in all establishments having over 30 permanent employees. The rights and duties of these councils are practically the same as those of the miners' councils.

The main purpose of the councils, however, is to bring the workmen in touch with the management; hence the councils are authorized by the law to submit plans for better, or more economical, or more practical management, and the employer is bound to consult them about the submitted plans. The employer is also expected to give the council an account of the financial condition and the prospects of the concern, and in establishments having at least 300 employees the council is entitled to demand a copy of the annual balance sheet. Conflicts between the council and the management are decided by a special committee, with the district judge acting as chairman.

Elections to these councils are governed by regulations similar to those provided for miners' councils. The council is elected for a period of one year, and all those who have been employed in the concern for at least one year are eligible.

Such are the main provisions of this law which marks a new era of democratic social policy, and introduces a new regulation of the wage system. In this peaceful way of social reforms, Czechoslovakia hopes to avoid violent social upheavals and to bring about social justice and peace.

XVI

SOCIAL WELFARE POLICY, AS SHOWN IN THE ASSISTANCE TO THE UNEMPLOYED, THE CARE FOR THE WAR SUFFERERS, AND SOCIAL INSURANCE

Dr. Jan Brabec, Councillor of the Ministry of Social Welfare

The independent State of Czechoslovakia was re-established at a time when the war fronts of the Central Powers had collapsed. The collapse brought about serious economic and social changes. It released a large mass of soldiers for whom employment could not be found at once, as the industries which had been working to supply the needs of the army now had to abandon that work and the shortage of raw materials made an early resumption of work for the needs of peace impossible.

There were large numbers of sick and wounded soldiers in the hospitals and out of them, and large numbers of widows and orphaned children of soldiers who had fallen in battle or died of disease, or had disappeared.

These conditions determined the first social welfare measures of the Government as regards aid from the funds of the State. As early at December 10, 1918, a law granting Government aid to the unemployed was passed by the National Assembly; a general law providing assistance to war sufferers was passed April 8, 1919. Social insurance is the third factor in the aid to persons lacking economic independence.

In this article the historical development of these three factors in the Czechoslovak Republic will be briefly sketched in this order:

1. Government aid to the unemployed.
2. Care for the war sufferers.
3. Social insurance.

I. Aid to the Unemployed

Under the law of December 10, 1918, aid was extended to demobilized soldiers and to persons who had been employed during the war and had to be insured against sickness (chiefly persons employed in industry and commerce). Benefits were paid at the rate of 4 crowns a day, occasionally at the sick-benefit rate (not exceeding 6 crowns a day); an additional payment of 1 crown a day was made for each dependent member of the household. The aggregate payment, including the family bonus, was not to exceed 10 crowns a day. The authority to grant benefits was vested in the so-called Demobilization Committees. Each county had its own Committee composed of an equal number of employers and employees. The applicant had to produce proof that he had made an unsuccessful application for work at a public employment bureau; he was bound to renew such application twice a week and to accept any suitable work assigned to him.

As the benefits thus granted were not directly productive economically, it was provided later by the law of October 17, 1919, that the county authorities might order the municipal corporations, the communes in particular, to undertake public works as an emergency measure to give work to the unemployed. The State would refund to the contractor two-thirds of the wages of such persons, not to exceed 6 crowns a day per worker. The power to allow benefits was transferred from the Demobilization Committees to the county authorities.

Refunds to employers represent a third method of aid to the unemployed. In order to prevent the dismissal of workers when production is stagnant the State refunds a certain proportion of the wages paid (say 70 per cent) to those employers who keep their workers employed.

The present legal status of the unemployed is based on the law of August 12, 1921, which provides a benefit of 8 crowns a day, increasing to 10 crowns in larger towns, and family bonuses of 2 crowns for the wife and 1 crown for each child under 14, the total payment not to exceed 16 crowns or, in larger towns, 18 crowns a day. The benefits are payable for six months, in exceptional cases for a year. It should be noted that workers idle as the result of a strike or lockout are not entitled to benefits, and that, in cases of reciprocity, benefits are paid also to citizens of other States.

The extent of Government aid to the unemployed may be judged from these figures: In 1919 more than 250 million crowns was paid out in benefits; in 1921 only 80 million crowns.

The present system of payments is to continue in

force until the end of 1922 at the latest. It will then be succeeded by the Ghent system under the law of July 19, 1921. The unemployment doles will then be paid through labor organizations, the State contributing, in principle, only as much as those organizations themselves.

II. Care for the War Sufferers

From the very beginning the Czechoslovak Government has recognized the principle that a systematic care for the war sufferers can only be undertaken by the State itself even if the private assistance of individuals and charitable organizations is not excluded.

The law of April 8, 1919, declared the chief obligations of the State in its care for the war invalids to be the following: To continue the medical and surgical treatment of the sick or wounded soldiers until their complete recovery; to provide them with prostheses and orthopedic apparatus when necessary; to educate the invalids for a suitable trade or calling according to their personal qualifications; to place them in a situation where they may successfully pursue their chosen trade or calling; to aid them financially in case of need and grant them regular allotments of money; to aid the dependent survivors of dead or missing soldiers.

As the first step the county authorities carried out a census of war invalids residing in the country (excepting salaried men and non-commissioned officers who, as professional soldiers, are under the juridiction and care of the Ministry of National Defense). A like census of war invalids resident abroad was carried out by representatives of the Czechoslovak Government in foreign countries. The proportionate reduction of the invalids' earning capacity was then ascertained through examinations by special mixed commissions.

Financial aid was granted to invalids for the purchase of machines and tools needed in their chosen trades, for the equipment of workshops and, in exceptional cases, also, for the furnishing of homes. The blind were provided with small homesteads—a home with a garden and a field where the invalid might live and partly earn his living. Some of the blind were placed in the tobacco stores as agents of the tobacco monopoly.

As the conditions in many trades are favorable for cooperative undertakings the Government aided the organization of cooperative societies of invalids for the manufacture of footwear, orthopedic apparatus, clothing, saddlery goods, etc. The societies would receive subsidies or non-interest bearing loans and would be aided to obtain raw materials and secure a share of Government orders.

After special provincial veterans' bureaus had been established at Prague (for Bohemia), Brno (for Moravia and Silesia), and Bratislava (for Slovakia and Carpathian Russia), the law of February 20, 1920, was passed providing for regular allotments of money to war sufferers. The basic allotments were moderate. An invalid, for example, whose earning capacity had been reduced at least 85 per cent would receive 1,800 crowns; a widow, 600 crowns; orphans, 300 crowns for the first child and 252 crowns for each of the others; parents, 300 crowns. The allotment would thus suffice for the absolute necessaries only, the veteran being required, so far as able, to obtain additional means by his own work. From this point of view all persons having an independent annual income of more than 4,000 crowns or earning more than 8,000 crowns by working for others were excluded from the benefits of the law, and allotments were to be granted only to invalids whose earning capacity had been reduced at least 20 per cent.

In the case of sickness the invalids, under certain conditions, are to receive medical assistance and medicines. When an invalid is being treated at a sanatorium at Government expense one-half of his allotment is paid to his family. The allotment may, under certain conditions, be capitalized in part or in full and converted into a lump sum so that the invalid may obtain sufficient means to engage in trade or business.

Widows unable to work and widows over 55 years of age were to receive an additional benefit of 120 crowns a year; in case of remarriage they were to receive a lump sum. Orphans were to receive allotments until they reached the 16th year of age. The allotments were increased 50 per cent to orphans who had lost both parents or were neglected by their mother.

By the law of January 25, 1922, the basic allotment to invalids whose earning capacity had been reduced at least 55 per cent was fixed at 2,400 crowns representing an increase of 600 crowns in the allotment to a total invalid. The minimum income excluding the invalid from the benefits of the law was raised to 6,000 crowns; the allotment to widows whose earning capacity had been reduced at least 50 per cent or who had to provide for at least two minor children was increased to 900 crowns.

The allotment to orphans was increased to 400 crowns a year and was to be paid to them until they completed their 18th year. The allotment to parents was likewise raised to 400 crowns, and the regulations concerning medical inspection and the granting of allotments were revised.

An additional 50 per cent cost-of-living bonus is at present paid with all allotments.

The extent of Government aid to war sufferers may best be judged from the fact that in the Czechoslovak Republic there are now about 170,000 war invalids, 110,000 widows, 180,000 orphans and 65,000 fathers and mothers of soldiers who have fallen in battle, died of disease, or are missing. In the budget for 1922 the expenditure for aid to the war sufferers is estimated at 500 million crowns.

III. Social Insurance

Social insurance, in principle, means the compulsory insurance of persons economically dependent against certain harmful social phenomena, particularly against sickness, injury, invalidity, and old age.

At the time the independent State of Czechoslovakia was reestablished social insurance in the country was represented chiefly by the insurance of industrial workers against sickness and injury, the pension insurance of the higher classes of private salaried employees, and the inadequate insurance of miners.

Attempts had been made in the old Austrian Empire to work out a complete system of workmen's insurance by the institution of insurance against invalidity and old age and later of a general social insurance, that is, a system that would protect not only dependent persons working for others but also certain classes of persons working independently, such as small business men and small farmers.

It was the first task of our State to revise the existing elements of social insurance and adapt them to the changed conditions, and also to unify the divergent legal provisions, for heretofore the old Austrian laws were in force in Bohemia, Moravia and Silesia while the old Hungarian laws prevailed in Slovakia and Carpathian Russia.

In the department of insurance against sickness the law of May 15, 1919, made compulsory the insurance of all persons performing labor or service on the basis of a contract of labor, service, or apprenticeship, as their chief and permanent occupation; all agricultural wage workers were thus included in the scope of the law.

The law also simplified the organization of sickness insurance by abolishing the small sick-benefit funds connected with individual establishments or societies and creating strong county funds.

The law of December 22, 1920, extended the term for which sick benefits might be granted to one year, at the same time increasing such benefits in accord with the readjustment of wage classes with higher earnings.

Women in childbed were allowed sick benefits for

six weeks before and six weeks after childbirth; compulsory insurance of family members was introduced, and the compensation for funeral expenses increased.

One-half of the insurance premium is to be paid by the person insured and one-half by the employer. The workers formerly paid two-thirds.

The maximum wage used as a basis for the calculation of benefits in the case of injury was raised to 6,000 crowns by amendments to the law regulating insurance against injury, adopted April 10 and October 29, 1919, and later to 12,000 crowns by the law of August 12, 1921, taking effect retroactively from January 1, 1921. The benefits payable to the injured workers or their survivors were supplemented by cost-of-living bonuses. The premiums for this class of insurance are paid by the employers exclusively.

The benefits payable by the fraternal funds of the miners were increased in a similar way by the law of October 29, 1919.

An amendment to the pension law adopted February 5, 1920, effected an increase of pensions through reclassification (wage classes up to 9,000 crowns). Compulsory pension insurance was extended, among other new classes, to the employees of commercial houses. The law also introduced preventive medical care, and collated the scattered provisions of the various acts then in force.

The pensions were supplemented by cost-of-living bonuses for the years 1920-22, the latest enactment being dated December 21, 1921.

The preliminary researches necessary for the working out of a complete system of social insurance have been entrusted to a special committee of experts in the Ministry of Social Welfare. The committee has adopted the following general principles:

Owing to fiscal reasons social insurance alone is to be maintained, a general system of national insurance not being feasible. For those same reasons the introduction of unemployment insurance must be postponed for the present and the Ghent system subsituted. In addition to the insurance of wage workers a plan is to be worked out for the insurance of certain classes of independent workers (small business men, small farmers). In all branches of social insurance for persons working for others the obligation to be insured shall be determined, so far as possible, by a uniform standard. The autonomy of the insurance funds is to be emphasized; a restriction of direct elections, however, would seem desirable in the interest of a stable administration of the funds. An adequate control of the funds by the State is likewise desirable.

No decisions have been made thus far as to the method of such Government control, or the quotas to be contributed by the insured and by the employers, respectively, as the committee awaits the final results of the census of February 15, 1921, particularly as regards the distribution of the population according to age, marital condition, and occupation.

By the law of December 21, 1921, the amount of 130 million crowns was appropriated for the purposes of social insurance for the period of transition which will require substantial contributions on the part of the State.

XVII

CHILD WELFARE

Dr. Jaroslav Janovský, Secretary in the Ministry of Social Welfare

The Czechoslovak Republic is one of the succession States of the former Austro-Hungarian Monarchy. That explains why the organization of child welfare institutions in the Republic is substantially a continuation of the legal status established by the laws formerly in force in Austria-Hungary. In this department of public administration, as in others, the laws of former Austria are still largely in force in Bohemia, Moravia, and Silesia, while the laws of former Hungary prevail in Slovakia and Carpathian Russia. A comprehensive general law for the protection of children, such as England, France and Belgium have enacted, is not to be found among the statutes of either Austria or Hungary. Provisions for the protection of children in our country have been incorporated gradually in the laws regulating the various departments of public life. The historical development of child welfare policies, and of the policy of social welfare in general, can be clearly traced in these successive Acts. As the idea gained ground that the protection of the destitute or dependent members of society was not the domain of charity alone but a direct duty of the State, the original scanty provisions of the family law and the law of guardianship—the earliest legal measures for the protection of children—were gradually supplemented by new enactments. The social protection of children thus passed from the confines of private law into various departments of public law, as the municipal corporations, the communes, and likewise the counties, the Provinces, and lastly the State itself, were now charged with the duty at public expense to maintain and educate children dependent on public aid.

From this point of view it may be said that the foundation for the public care of children in Bohemia, Moravia, and Silesia, the historic countries of the Bohemian State, was laid by the general Civil Code of 1811. The code granted to children a legal right to demand maintenance and education from their parents or other relatives, and charged the courts with duty to enforce that right and, when necessary, to make suitable provisions for the education of the children.

The various provisions of the Civil Code, and, in particular, those authorizing the courts to make suitable provisions for neglected children, naturally can be carried out only when certain institutions for the protection of children have been provided and the necessary funds are available. The latter needs have been taken care of by a series of laws including the general laws for the relief of the poor, the law of domicil of 1863 and its amendments of 1896, and the provincial Poor Law of Bohemia of 1868. By these laws the public care of the children is regulated in connection with the public relief of the poor, the practical application of the various provisions being entrusted to the self-governing administrative bodies, that is, the communes, the counties, and the Provinces. The counties and the Provinces are to contribute only in case the funds of the communes, or the counties, respectively, are insufficient for the performance of the duties entrusted to them under the Poor Laws. Under the Poor Laws of Bohemia the communes are bound to provide not only maintenance but also education for the children of the paupers domiciled therein; they are the chief factors responsible for the welfare of the children. Certain reforms contemplated in this connection will be discussed in the concluding part of this chapter dealing with poor relief.

Certain provincial laws regulating various special departments of child welfare under the authority of the Provinces cannot be noticed at length in this brief review. Two of the older laws still in force, which deserve a special mention, are the laws relating to workhouses and reformatories. These laws make it a duty of the several Provinces to establish and maintain reformatories and houses of correction for neglected children under 18 years of age, particularly for delinquent youths. The definition of neglected children as found in these laws is somewhat narrow, however. The Czechoslovak Ministry of Social Welfare has, therefore, prepared the draft of a law concerning protective education in which the educational provisions intended to safeguard the morals of the children are placed on a much broader and more solid basis. Under this bill a neglected minor below 18 years of age may, on an order of the judge of probate, receive education in a suitable institution or be placed with a private family, and the judge may issue such orders with or without the consent of the parents or legal representatives of the neglected children.

As a companion measure to this bill the Czechoslovak Ministry of Justice is preparing a reform of criminal jurisprudence in relation to juvenile delinquents. The criminal responsibility of minors is to begin only after they have reached the age of fourteen, and protective education or supervision may, in the case of youthful offenders, be substituted for punishment whenever the criminal judge shall deem such arrangement proper and sufficient.

Among the new child welfare laws which have been enacted since the organization of the Czechoslovak Ministry of Social Welfare special mention should be made of the law regulating child labor in connection with the general protection of wageworkers, and the law of June 30, 1919, for the protection of illegitimate children and children under the care of strangers. By the latter law public supervision has been extended to all children below 14 years of age living outside of their own family, and all illegitimate children.

An intensive development of child welfare legislation is to be expected when the public administration has been reorganized in accordance with the provisions of the Czechoslovak Constitution. The territory of the State is to be divided into 21 administrative districts, each of which will be sufficiently equipped, both financially and administratively, to perform its social welfare duties. The districts will, in case of need, receive subsidies from the State Treasury. Such is to be the general solution of the question of funds which often determines the success or failure of all social welfare laws.

The reorganization of the public administration in Czechoslovakia will make possible the fulfilment of another condition on which the success of child welfare institutions and laws may depend—the unification of legal and administrative procedure. In Slovakia and Carpathian Russia where the laws of former Hungary are in force the organization of the public care of children is somewhat different. In those Provinces the judicial supervision in matters of guardianship and tutelage has been entrusted to administrative organs, the orphans' tribunals, so-called, consisting of both official and lay members. The organization of poor relief is substantially the same as in the Bohemian countries; the communes may demand the aid of the larger administrative units (counties) in case their own funds are insufficient to assist the needy. In those territories children may be placed in State institutions or with private families, under the laws VIII and XXI of the year 1901.

It will be seen from the above that the Czechoslovak Administration considers it as its first duty to correlate the legal provisions for the protection of children, now scattered among the various departments of public and private law, and gradually to supplement them with new laws so as to place the public care of the children on a solid legal basis. At the same time, however, the Administration intends to conserve and develop the organization of private charities. In opposition to the idea of an exclusive State care of the children (a State monopoly of child welfare, so to speak) the Government has accepted the view that a rational care of the children requires the cooperation of official and voluntary agencies. With that purpose in view the Government has reorganized the existing charitable corporations which have reached a high degree of development (particularly the so-called provincial and county Child Welfare Commissions) so that they now embrace all institutions of this kind within their territorial jurisdiction. These corporations now act as advisers to public officials and occasionally assist in the execution of official decrees.

Relief of the Poor

The public relief of the poor in Czechoslovakia is based on the (imperial) law of domicil of 1863, as amended in 1896, and the provincial Poor Law of 1868 for Bohemia. Under these laws the communes are charged with the duty to maintain the local poor. It is a characteristic principle of the poor laws of Czechoslovakia that the claim for relief can be asserted against the community of the pauper's domicil only. The commune is accordingly bound, in principle, to support only those paupers who: (1) are domiciled therein; and (2) have no legal claim for maintenance against other persons and are not supported by a charitable society or institution; and (3) are unable to earn a living but will accept such employment as their home commune may offer them.

The law recognizes the following forms of poor

relief (a) the maintenance of persons unable to work; (b) the care of the sick; (c) the payment of funeral expenses; (d) the maintenance and education of children. The details of the organization of poor relief in the commune as well as the administration of the funds set aside for that purpose are left by the law to the discretion of the autonomous communal boards. Where the funds of the commune are insufficient the higher units of the public administration, the counties or the Province are to aid.

It is natural that after fifty years of operation the system of public relief of the poor in Czechoslovakia is in need of some reforms. It should be noted that the poor laws now in force were the result of social and economic conditions much more simple than those since produced by the rapid march of industrialization which has compelled a large majority of the citizens to earn their living outside the limits of the communes of their domicil. As a result the burden of poor relief is very unevenly distributed among the various communes. Thus the small communes in the less fertile regions where a large majority of the inhabitants can not make a living are much more burdened than others when they have to take care of their citizens who have emigrated to the industrial centers, or to maintain their children who may be total strangers to the residents. To remedy this inequality it is provided by the amendment of 1919 to the Communal Code that the communes are to be relieved of those burdensome duties, and the obligation to maintain the poor is to be placed on the higher administrative units or on the State.

XVIII

THE HOUSING QUESTION

Dr. Hynek Kubišta, Division Chief in the Ministry of Social Welfare

In the Czechoslovak Republic legislation dealing with the housing question is based on the housing laws of former Austria. In the Empire the State's interest in housing was chiefly fiscal, as evidenced by the high tax on rents. The first law designed expressly to improve the housing conditions—but only those of laborers—was the law of 1892 concerning sanitary and low-priced dwellings for workmen which was enacted for ten years, and re-enacted in 1902 for twenty years more. The first and only law of Austria which provided financial assistance to the builders of dwelling-houses was the law of 1910 establishing a State housing fund to promote the construction of small houses for people of moderate means, regardless of their occupation. The fund was to be used in part to guarantee mortgage loans granted to building societies or the communes and in part for direct building loans at low rates of interest. The advantages of this law were made use of mostly in the Czech territories where the cooperative idea was already firmly rooted especially among the workmen. Since 1908 there had existed in Austria a limited housing fund for the granting of direct loans for the building of homes for Government employees.

The expansion of building activities, especially on the part of the building societies, was promoted in no small measure by two laws of 1911 which offered special relief from taxation to the builders of small houses and effective relief from other taxes and assessments to building societies. During the World War, Austrian housing legislation was confined to a decree known as "Tenants' Protective Decree" and an ordinance designed to prevent reduction in the number of dwellings. The Hungarian housing laws, excepting the provisions for the protection of the tenants, were never very effective in the districts of Slovakia and Carpathian Ruthenia.

Czechoslovak housing legislation can be divided into three groups: The first contains ordinances and laws for the protection of the tenants; the second, the extraordinary housing provisions; and the third contains the laws for the promotion of building activity.

I. Law for the Protection of Tenants

The chief purpose of the ordinances and laws of this group was to limit the right of the owner to terminate a lease; then to restrict the right of the landlord to raise the rent of the old or the new tenant. The lease could be cancelled only for reasons stated in the ordinance. The rent could be increased only in the measure allowed by the ordinance. The guiding principle of the older provisions was that the net profits accruing from the rent should not be less than the profit received before the passage of the Rent Act. By the law of 1920, the landlord received the right to pass on to the tenants all the expenses of repairing the house and keeping it in good order.

The general increase of rents allowed by the new law is intended to compensate the landlord at least in part for the depreciation of the money. However, the old Rent Act also contained special provisions in favor of the landlords which worked, indirectly, of course, for the good of the tenants, too. Such were the provisions prohibiting an increase in the rate of interest charges on mortgage loans on rented houses. The loss suffered by the landlords through the general abrogation of the provisions mentioned above is balanced in the new law in such a way that the landlord can in certain cases compensate himself at the expense of the tenants. Furthermore, the new provisions of the Rent Act contain articles aimed against an improper sale of dwellings. The Rent Act originally applied only to small dwellings and stores, but was later extended to other dwellings and from 1920 to all rented rooms, commercial rooms, offices, meeting places, etc.

Hotels and new buildings, *i.e.,* houses built after the passage of the first Rent Act, have been excluded from the "tenants' protection" from the very beginning. By later provisions, railway-owned properties and stores in the renowned Czech resorts have also been excluded from the "tenants' protection." Leases can be terminated for weighty reasons only and with the consent of the court. The law states eleven reasons for which the court must give judgment for possession. The lease may be terminated at once without an order of ouster if the tenant commits waste causing considerable loss to the owner, or if the house has to be rebuilt on orders of the commissioner of buildings.

The basis for calculating the increase of the rent is the rate in force on the 1st of August, 1914, or that of the first lease after that date, the so-called "basic rent." The law of 1920 allowed an increase of 20 per cent in the basic rent. By the present law a general increase up to 60 per cent is allowed. The increase is graduated according to the size and the use of the rooms. For new tenants the regular increase is higher than for the old lessees. Besides this general increase in the rate which is not conditional on the permission of the court, the law further permits the landlords to raise the rent for any one of four special reasons: (1) increase in taxes; (2) increase in the expense of management and upkeep; (3) increase in the interest or other payments on mortgage debts; and (4) increase in the expenses for temporary or extraordinary repairs or restoration of the house. The consent of the court to the raising of the rent is required only in case the owner cannot agree on the rate with the tenant. The court decides whether, or in what measure, the increase of the rent is permissible, and, on investigation, will lower or raise the rent. The consequence of the provisions regulating the increase of rents is that the owners gradually improve their houses at the expense of the tenants.

The sub-tenant enjoys the same protection as the tenant against dispossession, and a stronger one against the increase in rent. The regulations relating to the termination of leases have had the desired results, but not so the regulations dealing with the increase of rents.

Their effectiveness depends on the cooperation of the tenants or subtenants, and consequently they cannot be effective when the tenant or subtenant fails to avail himself of them. From the point of view of the general welfare the effect of the "tenants' protection" has been, on the whole, beneficial. It is now the policy of the Government, however, to limit such protection to the most urgent cases only. The legislature as well as the Government are agreed that the owners of houses must be freed from the restrictions imposed on them under the extraordinary conditions prevailing during and after the war.

II. The Extraordinary Housing Provisions

It was foreseen that, in consequence of the World War, there would be a general shortage of housing accommodations during the war, and there were no means for making proper preparations to prevent such a calamity. The end of the war was sudden, demobilization was carried out speedily, and the demands of the public administration of the new State caused a considerable shifting of the population. During this general movement of the population there was in some towns such a shortage of housing accommodations that extraordinary measures had to be taken to prevent the destruction of public order. Meanwhile such measures had to be applied by which the most economical use could be effected of all rooms in buildings already standing which were suitable for dwellings. By the ordinance of January 22, 1919, and later by the act of October 30, 1919, municipalities suffering from a considerable shortage of housing accommodations were authorized to take over unused rooms for the housing of persons whose stay in the community was necessary for the public welfare, or who were domiciled there. Under these provisions unoccupied residences were taken over and used as dwellings, or for storage, commercial, manufacturing, farming, or studio purposes. When a person had more than one dwelling, the one which he did not use was taken over fcr occupation. Beside this, parts of large dwellings were also taken over in some cases. The municipalities were not allowed, however, to take over rooms used for educational purposes or in which artistic or other valuable collections were displayed, or rooms of artistic or historical value. The owners whose rooms had been taken over were compensated to the full amount of the rent. In accordance with these legal provisions tenants gladly rented such rooms which could be taken over as dwellings. In this way the housing accommodations were considerably enlarged. In Prague and its suburbs alone the number of dwellings thus acquired approximated 5,000. The number of the available rooms was exhausted very soon, however. The law providing for the taking over of unused rooms expired June 30, 1921, by limitation; by that time the foundations had been laid by special laws for the development of building activity.

The laws limiting the freedom of migration, namely, those of April 1, 1919, and of March 17, 1921, pursued the same aims as the law providing for the taking over of unused rooms by the muncipalities. In some towns where the shortage of housing accommodations was acute and the increase of population unusually large, only such persons were allowed to move in, up to the end of 1922, as were obliged to live there because of their profession, while other people could settle there only after having obtained official permission. The act of July 11, 1922, forbids the combination of two or more dwellings, hitherto separate, into one; forbids the possession of two or more dwellings; empowers the district authorities to compel the house-owner to rent rooms hitherto unrented which are suitable for dwellings; and provides that rooms may not be used for other than dwelling purposes save under an official permit. The law gives to the municipalities the right to control leases. The chapter of the law providing for dwellings for Government and railroad employees is of special importance.

III. Laws for the Promotion of Building Activity

After the World War, the building industries in Czechoslovakia were in a very unfavorable situation. As early as the beginning of 1919, the building costs were on the average four times higher than before the war, and at the end of 1919, ten times higher, while the income from the old houses as well as the new ones was, owing to the provisions of the Rent Act, almost on the same level as before the war. Building enterprises became the most unprofitable and unsafe. It was clear from the very beginning that building activity could not progress without public help. The Government therefore decided to grant financial assistance in the form of loan guaranty to building enterprises. By the Act of May 23, 1919, and later by the Act of February 20, 1920, the amounts of 5 and then 25 million crowns were set aside for buildings to be erected in 1919 or 1920. The money was to be used chiefly in aid of building societies in the form of Government guarantee of loans secured by a second mortgage on the house. The Government bound itself to the creditor of the guaranteed loan to pay the interest and amortization charges on the loan, if the rent of the house should not be sufficient. The Government, however, reserved for itself the control of the rent. The net result of both these laws was on the whole very slight. Demands made especially by the building organizations for Government assistance to private building enterprises were met by the Act of March 19, 1920, which allotted 250 million crowns in the form of subsidies for the erection of houses with accommodations for at least four families. The subsidy amounted to 40 per cent of the building costs. But this law failed also owing to the difficulties in getting the remaining 60 per cent not covered by the Government subsidy, and to the continual increase of the building costs in 1920.

Government assistance to building enterprises was not limited, however, to financial support only. Thus the laws providing relief for larger towns, passed in April and May, 1919, prescribed more economical and therefore less costly ways of building. By the Act of March 30, 1920, a total exemption from the house tax, rent tax and all surtaxes was granted to all new buildings erected by municipal corporations for a term of 20 years, and if the building had at least four dwellings, a permanent reduction amounting to one-fifth of the tax for the entire life of the house. The building activity of the communes and societies was stimulated by the Act of December 17, 1919, providing for the taking over of land for the erection of dwelling houses or public buildings. The activity of building enterprises was also quickened by various administrative orders and decrees especially by a reduction of railroad transportation rates for building materials, by a lowering of the prices of lumber, and by the control of the prices of other building materials, etc. However, in spite of all these laws and provisions for its promotion, the building activity did not keep pace with the shortage of housing accommodation and the need of keeping the building trades employed. In 1920 the cost of building was 16 times higher than before the war. The cause was, in the first place, the rise in the cost of living, the increase in wages, and the higher prices of building materials. The increase was caused in part by inefficiency in the production of building materials. The housing problem became so serious that the Government and the legislative bodies had to seek new ways for its solution. Two laws were passed: The law of March 3, 1921, and that of March 11, 1921, to stimulate building activity. The first law offered tax exemption to the builders of dwelling houses. Individuals paying the income tax or companies paying the profit tax were allowed to deduct 70 per cent of the construction costs of the new building from the basic taxable amount. Large industrial concerns took advantage of these savings on taxes in the building of new dwelling houses. The law of March 11, 1921, supplemented by the law of January 27, 1922, extended the right to acquire land under eminent domain to all builders of dwelling houses or business buildings.

The compensation for the land so acquired was to be based on the actual value of the land. The administrative officials directed the procedure for the acquisition of the land and determined the compensation to be paid. Arbitration courts were established for the settlement of wage disputes and other controversies in the building industry arising from the labor contracts, and for the regulation of the working conditions, especially in extraordinary cases not contemplated by the labor contracts. The employers were not allowed to dismiss workmen and the employees as well as their organizations were forbidden to strike while the court of arbitration was considering the matter in dispute. These regulations of the building industry were intended to stabilize wages and the working conditions. In a similar way the law provided for the establishment of price boards which were to fix the prices of building materials in order to put a stop to the continuous increases and work toward the stabilization of prices. The law of 1921 empowered the Government to obtain for the promotion of building activity the amount of one billion crowns by a lottery loan and to provide for the best employment of the proceeds. The Government was specially authorized to make use of 50,000,000 crowns from the proceeds of the lottery loan for the building of houses for Government employees.

As regards the financial assistance to be granted to building enterprises, the law enumerates six different kinds of such assistance: The guaranty of a loan; Government contribution toward the interest and amortization of the loan (in five years from 4 to 2.5 per cent of the building costs); the combination of the Government guaranty with a direct loan for the completion of the buildings started in 1919 and 1920 by municipalities or cooperative societies; finally, a contribution of 60 per cent of building costs, partly for temporary buildings, partly for buildings being put in order for occupancy, and partly for building space hitherto unoccupied. Houses with small apartments measuring at the most $80m^2$ of floor space will be exempt from the property tax and all other surtaxes for 50 years, other buildings for 20 years. In accordance with the law, assistance may be given to any builder and particularly to private persons. Until the end of August, 1922, assistance had been granted to the builders of 767 apartment houses with 6,814 apartments, and of 5,489 private houses with 6,342 dwellings, estimated to cost 1,197,387,058 crowns. At the end of 1921 there were completed and occupied 510 apartment houses with 6,788 apartments and 15,251 rooms, and 2,099 private houses with 2,579 dwellings of 6,640 rooms, with a building cost of 713,264,950 crowns. Besides that, at the end of 1921, there were in the process of construction 220 apartment houses with 2,344 apartments of 5,683 rooms and 2,093 private houses with 2,480 dwellings of 7,131 rooms, estimated to cost 490,814,160 crowns.

In 1922 the construction was begun of 349 apartment houses with 3,162 apartments and 3,013 private houses with 3,407 dwellings, estimated to cost 575,-962,037 crowns. At the end of 1922 the guaranteed loans on buildings already completed or in process of construction aggregated 1,390,000,000 crowns. The annual financial burden to the State from the guarantees amounts to about 100,000,000 crowns. By this contribution the Government has succeeded in mobilizing financial means amounting to more than 1,780 million crowns. Financial assistance to the building enterprises will decrease as the cost of building decreases. At the end of the 1922 building season the building costs were only eight times as high as before the war. It is expected that the continual decrease in the building costs will induce an extensive building activity even without Government support. The Government has not only promoted the building activity by its assistance to the municipalities, the building societies and private persons, but has also built houses for its own employees. Thus far the Government has built 118 apartment houses with 1,094 apartments and one dormitory with 118 beds at a cost of 152,371,000 crowns. Work has been commenced on the building of 114 apartment houses with 1146 apartments, to cost 120,000,000 crowns. These figures, however, do not include the houses and dwellings which some of the branches of the public administration, especially the railroad and the financial administration, have built for their employees.

In promoting the building activity as well as in building houses on its own account, the Government has always insisted that the new dwellings should offer all the comforts and conveniences provided by the modern art of the builder.

XIX

CRIME

Dr. August Miřička, Professor at the Charles University, Prague

In order to form a correct idea of the relative frequency of crime in the territories now forming the Czechoslovak Republic, it is necessary to investigate the conditions which existed there before and during the war and then to study the situation after the war.

Such a study obviously must be based on reliable statistical data. The State Statistical Bureau has collected statistics only for the Czech territories (Bohemia, Moravia and Silecia); the data for Slovakia and Ruthenia have not yet been compiled. According to the official census of February 15, 1921, the Czech territories exclusive of Slovakia and Carpathian Ruthenia had a population of 10,005,734.

Experience has demonstrated that after the outbreak of a war crime usually shows a decreasing tendency. That was the case in the Czech territories as early as 1914, although only a few months of that year had been taken up by the war. Table I shows a decrease in criminal cases (felonies and misdemeanors) from 32,043 in 1912 and 34,465 in 1913 to 33,154 in 1914 and to 26,595 in 1915. There is also a corresponding decrease in the number of persons indicted and convicted. In 1912 there were 14,348 indicted of whom 11,281 were convicted (of these 8,054 of felony); in 1914 there were only 13,003 indictments and 9,776 convictions (6,678 of felony); and in 1915 there were but 11,541 indictments and 8,177 convictions (6,362 of felony). In petty offenses a similar decrease is to be observed in the years 1914 and 1915 as shown in table II.

I. PROCEEDINGS IN COURTS OF FIRST INSTANCE

Year	No. of cases	No. of persons accused	No. of persons indicted	Total No. of persons convicted	No. of persons convicted of felony
1919	32,043	82,210	14,348	11,281	7,914
1913	34,465	86,652	14,873	11,837	8,054
1914	33,154	79,214	13,003	9,776	6,678
1915	26,593	76,028	11,541	8,177	6,362
1916	27,704	84,287	12,289	8,581	6,124
1917	40,691	130,461	17,470	11,876	8,903
1918	49,517	187,449	25,153	16,673	13,509
1919	60,166	220,349	33,694	20,776	17,253
1920	96,959	253,710	50,294	32,991	26,640

II. PROCEEDINGS IN THE COUNTY COURTS

Year	Total No. of cases	No. of cases prosecuted by private parties	No. of persons convicted
1912	326,017	83,391	150,191
1913	334,611	84,409	153,664
1914	296,171	67,111	136,725
1915	269,866	54,504	120,700
1916	245,328	32,625	109,699
1917	261,717	36,369	111,066
1918	215,742	42,785	86,677
1919	268,463	62,904	110,213
1920	295,722	75,204	133,027

Many criminologists and sociologists who have studied the relation between war and crime have tried to explain the interesting fact that the outbreak of war is usually followed by a decrease of crime. It might be expected that in a war when economic values and even human life are considered of little importance, crime would increase rather than decrease. The decrease of crime in war as shown by official statistics, is often explained, especially by German writers, by the assumption that war has an ennobling influence on man, as it turns all thoughts and efforts of the citizens to the noble struggle for the victory of the fatherland.

In the "Zeitschrift fuer die gesamte Strafrechtswirtschaft" (vol. 43, page 402), Professor Hippel explains the decrease in the number of persons convicted of crime in Germany in 1914 as follows: "The decrease is explained by the five months of war. It shows a vigorous people in arms. The men fit for military service are at the front, while discipline and order rule at home."

However, such an explanation will not hold good for the territories inhabited by Czechoslovaks who felt no enthusiasm for the war. To me such an explanation of the decrease in crime seems rather idealistic: I think that we must look for a more sober explanation. Large numbers of men of the age which, in normal times, furnishes the greatest number of criminals, are called to arms and thus forced into a life which affords far less opportunity for the commission of criminal offenses. When, however, offenses are committed, they do not appear in the official statistics because they are punished by military courts and consequently are not included in the official statistics of crime. Moreover, criminals under indictment are also called to the colors, and judges, too, must join their regiments. Thus many trials have to be deferred. The fact that an offense has been committed is therefore not shown in the statistics for the year in which it has been committed, but only in the statistics of some later year.

The decrease in the first two war years was followed by a marked increase in crime. This increase became evident as early as 1916, when there were 27,704 cases, 12,289 indictments and 8,581 convictions (6,124 of crime). In the following years the increase was still greater: In 1917 there were 11,876 convictions (8,903 of crime), in 1918 16,873 convictions (13,509 of crime). As can be seen from these figures, the number of offenses committed in the years 1919 and 1920 was much larger than in the prewar years.

This larger postwar increase of crime in the Czech territories, especially after the Revolution of 1918, would have to be considered a serious menace if the abnormal postwar conditions were not taken into account. There are certain general causes which are responsible for the increase of crime after every war, and which have doubtless brought about an increase in crime in other countries also. These causes are naturally the more effective the longer the war has lasted. The demoralizing effects of the war both at the front and at home, the low passions unleashed by the war, and the general decline in the valuation of human life are chiefly responsible for the increase in crime. In the victorious countries, too, we may observe a spiritual exaltation which sometimes reaches the stage of frenzy and, when stimulated by alcohol, frequently finds expression in deeds of violence. It is a well-known fact that after the Franco-Prussian war of 1870-71, the number of crimes against the person and crimes of violence in general increased considerably in Germany.

Any conclusions in this direction, with regard to the present, can be made only on the basis of a detailed classification of the total number of crimes and offenses. The publication of the State Bureau of Statistics contains, however, only a partial classification, that is, only a classification of those penal offenses which are included in Tables III (crimes) and IV (petty offenses). (See page 244.)

Those committing two or more delicts are counted for each offense.

If we divide the crimes included in Table III into two major groups, one consisting of crimes against the person (crimes against chastity, murder, infanticide, manslaughter, and mayhem) and the other of crimes against property (arson, larceny, embezzlement, robbery, and fraud), we see at once that the offenses of the first group show, in some cases, a remarkable decrease as compared with the number of cases before the war, especially in the case of mayhem, of which there were 933 and 846 cases in the years 1912 and 1913, but only 208 and 328 in 1919 and 1920. In the case of crimes against property, however, with the exception of arson, a marked increase is to be noted.

The greatest increase is in the case of larceny and receiving stolen goods. The causes of this increase are to be found in the demoralization of the people by the long war and the economic crisis and unemployment.

III. NUMBER OF PERSONS CONVICTED OF CRIME

Year:	Total	Crimes against chastity	Murder	Infanticide	Manslaughter	Mayhem	Arson	Grand larceny	Embezzlement	Robbery and burglary	Fraud
1912	7,914	443	38	3	47	933	41	2,553	231	48	798
1913	8,054	418	28	3	33	846	34	2,750	256	39	721
1914	6,678	418	33	19	50	660	39	2,464	216	48	691
1915	6,362	277	27	15	21	252	29	2,927	178	38	549
1916	6,124	196	16	10	24	180	28	4,011	145	14	567
1917	8,903	107	11	11	3	125	4	7,007	107	14	652
1918	13,509	65	18	2	9	135	12	11,164	153	21	917
1919	17,253	98	36	6	28	208	13	14,703	236	85	868
1920	26,640	211	46	15	28	328	15	21,389	767	111	1,657

IV. NUMBER OF PERSONS CONVICTED BY THE COUNTY COURTS OF PETTY OFFENSES

Year	Assault & battery	Petty larceny & complicity	Embezzlement	Fraud	Buying of stolen goods	Pandering	Drunkenness	Begging & Vagrancy
1912	26,997	37,540	2,981	6,264	1,131	150	332	48,666
1913	28,807	38,575	2,804	5,834	148	137	295	47,844
1914	33,391	37,753	2,562	5,079	905	154	313	49,520
1915	13,230	38,467	2,014	3,709	1,330	126	151	33,444
1916	9,657	39,604	1,753	3,217	1,572	119	89	21,014
1917	6,933	56,769	1,611	2,694	2,284	60	31	13,885
1918	5,779	46,818	1,261	1,909	3,046	46	27	7,784
1919	9,089	49,324	1,556	2,523	3,283	46	172	11,553
1920	14,303	56,303	1,668	3,337	3,715	40	308	14,382

These causes have doubtless brought about an increase in offenses against property in other countries also. But they alone cannot explain the large increase in theft after the war in the Czechoslovak territories as compared with the number of thefts before the war. Here the explanation lies in a peculiar modification of the criminal law. Under the law, the value of the stolen goods determines the nature of the offense, whether it is a felony or merely a misdemeanor. If the value of the stolen article is over 200 crowns, or if the act is done under certain aggravating circumstances defined by the law, in which case the value may be only over 50 crowns, the offense is classed as grand larceny. With the decrease in the value of the Czechoslovak crown the prices of commodities have increased many times, but the law defining the difference between grand and petty larceny has not been changed. That explains the large increase during the years 1919 and 1920, when the number of the cases of grand larceny was almost eight times as great (21,389) as in 1913 (2,750), while the number of petty thefts was less than twice as large as in 1913 (56,303 against 38,575).

Austria-Hungary had passed strict laws to stop war profiteering. After the war the penalties had to be made more severe as the offenses were on the increase. This was accomplished by special statutes (Law of October 17, 1919, Nos. 567-568 of the Collection of Laws and Government Decrees, and Law of March 18, 1921, No. 129) modifying not only the substantive law (increase of penalties, exclusion of extraordinary leniency or conditional conviction, possibility of confiscation of property, hard labor), but also the rules of procedure. For the prosecution of war profiteers special tribunals were established consisting of professional and lay judges, the latter being selected from a list of persons submitted by trade unions, or by organizations of different groups of producers and consumers. This was done in order to place the prosecution of the war profiteers in the hands of the people themselves.

This arrangement has not been very satisfactory in practice. The lay judges especially have been criticized for having no interest in the prosecution, or showing partiality in their decisions, or hampering the administration of justice by non-attendance at trials. Thus these special courts have failed to win the confidence of the public; the producers and the merchants complain of unjustifiable persecution, while the consumers charge the courts with being too lenient in prosecuting the war profiteers.

According to the statistics compiled by the Ministry of Justice for the Czech territories (Bohemia, Moravia and Silesia) 100 complaints of war profiteering crimes were filed in 1921, and about 7,400 complaints of misdemeanors, 23,000 complaints of petty offenses punishable summarily by the courts and about 16,000 complaints of petty offenses punishable by administrative authorities. Only 18 of the criminal profiteers were indicted for a felony, and 3,500 for a misdemeanor, but less than 50 per cent of the offenders were convicted. Summary convictions for petty offenses of profiteering numbered only a little more than 3,000.

The small number of 18 indictments for felony shows that the law did not reach the big profiteers but only their petty imitators, against whom it was easy to obtain evidence. The decreasing number of complaints in cases of war profiteering, as well as of convictions as compared with acquittals, shows that with the return of normal economic conditions and the restoration of competition the laws against war profiteering are gradually losing their importance. Modification of these laws is being considered, and the time of their repeal is not far off.

The young Republic had to protect its citizens not only against wild speculation in necessaries, but also against the illegal exportation of goods needed at home. A law against clandestine exports was passed in March 18, 1920 (No. 188 of the Collection of Laws and Government Decrees); in point of severity it may be compared with the laws against war profiteering. To safeguard the confidence of the public in the currency, the Parliament passed a new law providing for the punishment of persons guilty of counterfeiting money or securities (Law of May 22, 1919, No. 269 of the Collection of Laws and Governmental Decrees).

The obsolete criminal laws of former Austria require an early revision. A revision is also necessary to provide a uniform code of law for the Republic, for the old Hungarian laws are still in force in Slovakia and Carpathian Ruthenia. By various measures the Government has endeavored to modernize the penal system and to establish new institutions for the reformation of the criminals. Thus, by the Law of October 17, 1919 (No. 564 of the Collection of Laws and Governmental Decrees) a probation system was introduced and conditional suspension of the sentence was authorized.

The Government also intends to establish juvenile courts modeled on those originated in the United States of America which have been adopted by many European countries.

A thoroughgoing reform of the penal code which will establish a modern and uniform system of criminal jurisprudence throughout the Republic is now in the process of preparation.

INDEX